crossroads

a step-by-step guide away from addiction

facilitator's guide

Edward T. Welch

New
Growth
Press

WWW.NEWGROWTHPRESS.COM

New Growth Press, Greensboro, NC 27404
Copyright © 2008 by Edward T. Welch

Unless noted otherwise, all Scripture quotations are from the New International Version, copyright © 1973, 1978, 1984 by International Bible Society.

The other Bible quoted is English Standard Version (ESV), the Holy Bible, English Standard Version, copyright © 2001 by Crossway Bibles, a division of Good News Publishers.

ISBN: 978-1-934885-93-2

Library of Congress Cataloging-in-Publication Data
Welch, Edward T., 1953–
    Crossroads : a step-by-step guide away from addiction : facilitator's guide / by Edward T. Welch.
        p. cm.
    ISBN 978-1-934885-93-2 (pbk.)
    1. Compulsive behavior—Religious aspects—Christianity. 2. Compulsive behavior—Rehabilitation. 3. Addicts—Rehabilitation. 4. Recovering addicts—Religious life. 5. Church group work. I. Title.
    BV4598.7.W44 2008
    248.8629—dc22

                                                                2008041208

Printed in India

27 26 25 24 23 22 21 20   8 9 10 11 12

CONTENTS

FOR FACILITATORS AND FRIENDS

TO WALK WITH AN ADDICT is both a gift and a grief. It is a privilege to bear another's burdens and love someone who is, in most ways, just like you. But it is painful to be lied to, to witness the ups and downs, and to watch while someone you love trashes his or her life and the lives of other people. These challenges are enough to lead you into humility and prayer, which are exactly the basic requirements for the job. Add love and you have the whole package.

A wise old ex-addict, a man who had come alongside hundreds of other addicts over the course of his sobriety, was asked how he could keep doing it when so many seemed to go back to their addictions. "I want to love them well," he said. "Then, when they are ready to change, they will remember that there is at least one person who cares, and they can call me."

That sounds pessimistic, but it actually points to a no-lose proposition. When you love someone who struggles with an addiction, you may end up watching that person disappear back into addiction. If that happens, you pray for another opportunity. Or you may see the Spirit of God work in that person's life. Either way, you were a faithful ambassador for Jesus Christ.

Love, humility, and prayerfulness—wrapped together with a confidence that God speaks with authority and grace to the difficult problem of addictions—are the basic requirements for the job. They all go together. If you have one, the others follow. If you are prayerful about another person, you will grow in humility because prayer says, "I need Jesus." You will also grow in love because you can't help but love someone for whom you consistently pray.

Of the three, love is the best summary of your job description. So, do you love well? Do you love in such a way that the struggling person knows that you love him or her? If you do, you are already going to help more than any manual or study guide. Of course, the Spirit of God can use all kinds of means to bring change in other people's lives, but, more often than not, the Spirit uses love.

Consider *Crossroads* a supplement to your ministry of wise love. Here is an overview of what is ahead:

- The steps in *Crossroads* try to mimic the way Jesus speaks to us.
- They speak in a direct, no-nonsense style.
- They ask questions as a way to teach and lead.
- They surprise or, even better, amaze.
- The steps in *Crossroads* provide warnings.
- They point out the path of beauty and lasting satisfaction.
- They bring hope on every page because all of God's words to the addict are summed up in the good news given to us by Jesus Christ. His love cannot be turned away, and his power can release anyone from bondage.

You, too, will adopt these different styles at different times. Love has rich variety.

The title *Crossroads* comes from one of the recurring images in the book. When we read through Proverbs, we notice that we are always standing at a crossroads, with Wisdom pointing us to the Kingdom of Heaven and Folly trying to seduce us away from it. At that decision point, which we encounter all the time, we must be wide awake, all our wits about us, because our natural instinct is to veer onto the path of folly.

When seen from a distance, folly looks like—well, folly. After all, who would tease an asp or walk randomly around an area loaded with traps and snares? But when temptation is breathing down our necks, it can suddenly appear rational, attractive, and satisfying. One goal of the Book of Proverbs is to prepare us for that crossroads moment by helping us take a step back, get a little distance.

Other images run through the book as well: light, darkness, wilderness journeys, and banquets. Any of them could be the organizing theme, but "crossroads" is flexible enough to incorporate a wide swath of the biblical teaching.

A WORD ABOUT METHOD

The workbook, of course, is unapologetically God oriented and Christ focused. This might be too much for someone who is committed to discovering his or her own god rather than knowing God-who-has-revealed-himself-as-THE-God. But it should suit most addicts just fine. Those who have a difficult time saying no to temptations know they need help. They know they need God. Usually they prefer that the knowledge of God not be left to their own judgment. They know the real thing when they hear it.

In the table of contents, you will notice that the steps specifically about God don't come until the middle of the book. This gives addicts time to see themselves more accurately before they really consider the character of God. For example, if an addict believes that his or her problem is largely biological, God will be a healer and helper, but he won't be the crucified Redeemer. Start with people and move toward God, or start with God and then talk about people—the knowledge of one is always connected to the other. You could start either place. I have chosen to show addicts their needs first, then move into the specifics of how God in Christ meets those needs.

A WORD ABOUT LANGUAGE

Use the word *addiction* with caution, or at least with self-awareness. We inject words with particular meanings. Your goal is to supply meaning that will easily draw a person into the story of Scripture. In the pop psychology of our times, the word *addiction* means so many different things that it can easily remain outside of the biblical story. But if you reload the word so that it means temptation, desires run amok, or voluntary slavery, then Scripture comes alive.

Most words are neither good nor bad. But some words and their meanings are more easily assimilated by Scripture, and some tend to resist biblical oversight. You, of course, want addicts to find themselves on every page of Scripture. To that end, you will be alert to words such as *addictions* and *cravings* that, though they can be easily understood biblically, take some extra work to establish the links. The method you use to bring all things under the oversight of God's Word can be flexible. Some people prefer to define terms up front. Others prefer to let Scripture gradually demonstrate its interpretive power.

OFFERING HOPE

All the basics should be here: reading Scripture, prayer, confession, and hope through knowing Jesus Christ and responding to him. The means of change for addicts are the same as they are for everyone else. To go in search of a new strategy to deal with addictions would be to say that God has not said enough to us in Scripture. Your job, ultimately, is to help the members of your group see that there is genuine hope and freedom in the gospel of Jesus Christ. A big part of that will be helping them to see where God is *already* at work in their lives. So be alert: watch for evidence of progress, and encourage your group members by telling them what you see.

One last thing: all of the material from your group members' guides is the main text here in this facilitator's guide. The leader-specific material in this guide is set off by an arrow. You will notice that they get less frequent as the book progresses. That is intentional: as you get deeper into this study, you as the study leader won't need my guidance as much. Or rather, you need God-given discernment more than you need any additional guidance you could get from a leader's note. Every group is different, and members will progress at different rates. As you moderate the discussion, pray for wisdom and discernment to see how best to offer hope to the members of your group.

Crossroads will give you the opportunity to be a blessing to people who need the hope that God offers in Christ. And you can expect to be blessed yourself as you see God's faithfulness at work.

A FEW PRELIMINARIES

GROUPS ARE LIKE A SMALL CHURCH. In the simple act of meeting together, men and women are saying that they need help. Without the help of Scripture and other people, they lose their way and go blind to the mixed motives of their hearts. When men and women attend a group, they are making a step of humility, which is a wonderful and necessary first step when attacking any addiction.

Meeting together is normal—lots of people do such things. But it is also extraordinary. You are meeting in the name of Jesus; you are meeting in order to know Jesus. That alone is dramatic evidence that God is on the move, and you have the opportunity to remind men and women of that spiritual reality. Be sure to let them know: their presence in the group is evidence of God's power and love for them.

The structure of a group can vary. If you are meeting with only one other person, you will have less structure. You could use this book as a guide for discussion. Read together parts that either of you highlighted. When something doesn't make sense, pray for wisdom.

> If any of you lacks wisdom, he should ask God, who gives generously to all without finding fault, and it will be given to him. (James 1:5)

The larger the group, the greater the need for some structure. Senates have their parliamentary procedures, committees their Robert's Rules of Order, and teachers their lesson plans and classroom rules. For those who struggle with addictions, structure can help because addicts, once they start talking, have a lot to say.

There can be a designated leader or rotating chairpersons, and the order of the meeting can vary, depending on the interests and needs of the group. It can include any of the following:

- A predetermined time to start and stop
- A statement of purpose—this is a nice opportunity for you to consider why you are meeting together and put that into words.

Aim to be brief. For example, "We need help, God gives help, and he uses people."

- Prayer
- A short passage of Scripture that is relevant to the meeting's topic
- A testimony. Consider ending the testimony by asking the person how the group can pray for him or her, but be careful to keep the time from being a group counseling session. It is hard enough to share something shameful, such as an addiction. An advice free-for-all could be confusing at best and could easily push the person away. If the person has no accountability partner, you could talk after the meeting and suggest someone who could be a mentor.
- A brief summary about the step discussed in the meeting
- Group responses, action plans, or questions about the step. Keep comments brief.
- Prayer for one another. In a large group, you could write requests for prayer on a 3x5 card and distribute them to group members.
- A hymn
- A benediction. One of the shocking things about God is that he desires to bless his people. The blessing from Number 6:24–26 is one example.

"Getting Started" is a step. Have your friend or friends (let's use "friend" rather than "addict") read aloud the parts that are particularly relevant. They can insert brief commentary.

GETTING STARTED

DO ANY OF THESE STATEMENTS FIT?

- You feel out of control. What began as an escape from the hassles of life has become hazardous. Something—drugs, alcohol, gambling, food, sex—is taking over. You feel like its slave.
- You still love your addiction, but it is no longer friendly. You think it is time for a change.
- You think it is time for change—you want to leave your addiction—but you aren't sure how to change. You have already tried a few strategies, and they didn't work.
- Someone told you that you'd *better* change.
- You are sick and tired of the lies, broken relationships, and nagging conscience that accompany all addictions.
- You are already off and running, already leaving your addiction behind.

Whichever fits, welcome to reality. You are closing in on it.

▷ Reality = life as God interprets it.

Reality is not as bad as you think. Yes, the world around you can be miserable at times. It can be miserable *most* of the time, as a matter of fact. You have known that misery. Otherwise, you wouldn't have preferred an altered reality. But there is more to reality than what you see. Usually you are looking through glasses that are smudged, scratched, and out of focus, and things don't look good. But reality—true reality—is better than you think.

Your addiction has taken you to the woodshed for a good whuppin'. At those times it is hard to see hints of beauty, goodness, justice, love, and joy, that are always peeking out of this life, but they are still there.

Let me put it this way: What if you were invited to the greatest feast ever? What if you received a promise of great treasure? Would that be enough to lure you away from an addictive way of life? It, at least, would get your attention.

> It is never too soon to entice someone with a new vision of wonderful things. Read the first nine chapters of Proverbs, and you will find a series of warnings and inducements, all given by a wise man who is savvy about the human heart. All these inducements find their fullest expression in the gospel of Jesus Christ.

Think of this book as a treasure map. At times you are reluctant to give up your addiction, in which case a map, even a map to someplace beautiful, isn't powerful enough to guide you. Yet at other times you are sick and tired of being owned by something that is killing you, and you are ready to leave it behind. The problem at those times is that you simply don't know how to get away. Every trail seems to loop right back to where you began. It is as though the object of your addiction sucks you into its gravitational pull and there is no defense against it. The purpose of the steps ahead is to orient you and direct you to a path of change that has been proven to transform people.

> This, of course, is not to tout *Crossroads* as the answer. God's Word, applied by his Spirit, transforms.

A few points before you get started.

First, *your struggle is a common one.* Don't begin with the idea that your experience is out of the ordinary. It is, of course, unique—no one completely understands your struggle (not even you). Still, we are all cut from the same cloth. All of us, if we are truly honest, would have to acknowledge a familiarity with that tug of addictions. A lot of *wanting* is in the human heart.

> This is self-evident: addicts want more. But this is also a radical statement that cuts across the grain of much of the teaching on addiction. Addicts are victimized by addictions, but they also want them. Their hearts are always active.

The desire for drugs, alcohol, sex, and food are the more dramatic ones, but they aren't fundamentally different from our cravings for comfort, significance, relationship, money, love, and so on. Try to find one person who has successfully and consistently said no to any of those wants. You won't succeed.

If you consider yourself a special case—the worst addict, the most victimized—stop and think about what you are really saying. Right below the surface is the idea, *Whatever worked for other people is not going to work for me.* And right below that idea is the private thought, *I am not going to change.*

You might be saying, "I *can't* change." You are afraid to get your hopes up for what could be another failure. Or you might be saying, "I *won't* change." You virtually dare people and programs to take their best shot at you so you can show them that they are not as good as advertised. Either way, you have already decided that nothing will help. You are certain that you are not normal, so normal treatments (this book, for instance) won't help. You may genuinely hope that *something* will come along and be the answer, but you suspect it never will.

> Voluntary slavery is one of the paradoxes of the human heart that is apparent in addiction. This paragraph, again, emphasizes the **voluntary** nature of the heart.

If that's you—if you believe that your case is unique—perhaps you still love your addiction more than you love anything else. That doesn't mean that a guide such as this is a waste of time. It just means that you are starting at a disadvantage.

> This sounds blunt, but addicts don't mind your being blunt. They mind hypocrisy, and they mind bluntness without love, as they should.

Second, *the path you will be traveling has much to do with God.* That should come as no surprise. Books about addictions always say something about God. But much more is happening between you and God than you may think.

- You will be surprised to learn how you avoid him.
- You will be surprised to learn how he pursues you.
- You will be surprised that you know him more than you think.
- You will be surprised that you know him less than you think.

> Addicts have a tendency to be numb. "Surprise" might rouse them. Also, it is a reminder that you don't want to say things that seem worn out and predictable. You will be considering the words of Christ, and they are the words of a cosmic revolution.

If you find yourself shutting down when the conversation turns to God, don't just wait for the conversation to move to something else. When you shut down at the mention of someone's name, the issue is *not* that he is irrelevant to you. The issue is that he is more relevant to you than you are comfortable with. Take a quick look, and you will probably find a history of misunderstandings and fractures in the relationship. Your addictions are linked to your relationship to God more than you realize. You can't ignore that.

Third, if at all possible, *do this work with someone else.* Addictions are private, so doing this in public is a way to take a stand against your addiction. God has always planned for people to live and grow in a community, where we give and receive, pray for others and get prayed for, and learn wisdom and offer it.

This book has its roots in a book called *Addiction—A Banquet in the Grave.*

This book overlaps with **Crossroads**. It would be worthwhile for you to read.

The image of the banquet comes from the Book of Proverbs. Just insert "Addiction" for "The woman Folly" and it will make sense.

The woman Folly [Addiction] is loud;
    she is undisciplined and without knowledge.
She sits at the door of her house,
    on a seat at the highest point of the city,
calling out to those who pass by,
    who go straight on their way.
"Let all who are simple come in here!"
    she says to those who lack judgment.
"Stolen water is sweet;
    food eaten in secret is delicious!"
But little do they know that the dead are there,
    that her guests are in the depths of the grave.
               (Proverbs 9:13–18, emphasis added)

Vivid, accurate, and tragic. Addictions lure you.

This emphasizes the slavery side of voluntary slavery.

They look attractive until the lights are turned on and you see the ugliness, horror, and death swirling around you. This is not the banquet you were hoping for.

But Dame Folly's banquet in the grave isn't the only banquet. There is another one. *The* God has invited you to *The* Banquet. This banquet is in his honor, and he has picked up the tab so you can come.

Who would have thought? The treatment for addictions is to want something better than your addictions.

> "Come, all you who are thirsty,
>   come to the waters;
>   and you who have no money,
>   come, buy and eat!
> Come, buy wine and milk
>   without money and without cost.
> Why spend money on what is not bread,
>   and your labor on what does not satisfy?
>   Listen, listen to me, and eat what is good,
>   and your soul will delight in the richest of fare."
>   (Isaiah 55:1–2)

Inviting, isn't it?

⇨ The gospel is a universal invitation. The simple requirement for this banquet is that you bring nothing. You acknowledge your need for Jesus and believe that he is, indeed, the risen Lord who has paid everything on your behalf. Does anyone think he or she is too bad and unworthy to come? The invitation is especially directed to the marginalized and unworthy, such as murderers (King David), adulterers (King David again), liars (the apostle Peter), and all others who have nothing to bring.

STEP 1:

Listen

MAIN IDEA: The path away from addiction begins by waking up and listening, really listening. Such listening also goes by another name: it is called humility.

> For background reading, consider chapters 1–3 of *Addictions—A Banquet in the Grave.*

The rumors are true. There really is a way through the addictive fog. When you consider the number of times you tried to stop and then went back to your addiction, you can easily believe that life is a revolving stage, always returning to the same place.

> Scripture is quite realistic when it comes to addictions (Proverbs 23:29–35). Addicts can be like dogs that return to their vomit (Proverbs 26:11). By stating the obvious about addictions, you are creating a culture where men and women can speak openly about their struggles. That alone can be hopeful, and hope is what you are offering.

But there really is a guidebook to life, and, contrary to what you think, it is available to everyone, including you.

> Wisdom calls aloud in the street,
>   she raises her voice in the public squares;
> at the head of the noisy streets she cries out,
>   in the gateways of the city she makes her speech.
>   (Proverbs 1:20–21)

Wisdom means knowing how life is supposed to work—how it works best. To get it, you just have to listen.

TWO VOICES

But listening to Wisdom is not that easy. As you know, another voice calls out in the street. That voice is Folly.

> Here is the crossroads we all face.

Folly. Folly—also known as Addiction—offers the flash and cash. Consider what she promises, and it's no wonder she is difficult to resist:

- Something secret
- Quick money
- Pleasure
- Rest, relaxation, and ease
- No problems (at least for right now)
- "Friends" who will encourage you in your foolish path

It's what she *doesn't* say that is the killer.

She cries out, "Now! Now! Now! You can have all this now!" Who wouldn't listen to such a promise even if she hasn't delivered? But here is reality. Her speech is a trap that is barely camouflaged. As she invites you to her banquet, she tries to shield your eyes from the death all around you. The stench is masked by cheap perfume. Even while you become contaminated, as the disease spreads and your own flesh begins to rot, she promises that *more* of your addiction is the only tonic that will heal. Death is her trade. Lies are her native tongue.

> These warning images come from Proverbs 9. Warnings are not con-
> demnation. Don't be afraid to offer warnings; when you love someone
> you want to scare them away from death and induce them to life.

Wisdom. It would be nice if you could simply say, "Oops, I lost my way," then start following the voice of wisdom. But as you know, the work in front of you will be a battle. Think of the cartoons where a person has two miniature creatures—a "Mini-Me" on each shoulder—whispering in either ear: foolishness in one ear and wisdom in the other. Foolishness usually wins. Foolishness is the hip contrast to wisdom. Who wouldn't follow it? From a distance, foolishness sounds ridiculous. It makes promises it can't keep, and it has nothing to give except death anyway. But close up, when it conjures up a mirage that matches our desires, foolishness sounds like life itself.

> From a distance versus up close—that will be an important distinc-
> tion. Perhaps the addictive object is temporarily out of reach, and your
> friends have a false sense of power and clarity. They should remem-
> ber that when the object of their affection comes close, they could
> easily go temporarily insane. It is time to be afraid and get prepared.

Wisdom, or at least the stereotype of it, seems boring by compari-son. Slow and steady. How many ways can you make "Don't do it"

sound interesting? But wisdom doesn't just fade away when it loses to
the slick appeal of foolishness. Instead, wisdom goes into overdrive. It
speaks more beautifully, exposes the ugliness of folly, and makes promises that it will keep. Wisdom woos you. It beckons. It persuades.

Do not forget my teaching,
    but keep my commands in your heart,
for they will prolong your life many years
    and bring you prosperity. (Proverbs 3:1–2)

"Lay hold of my words with all your heart;
    keep my commands and you will live.
Get wisdom, get understanding;
    do not forsake my words or swerve from them.
Do not forsake wisdom, and she will protect you;
    love her, and she will watch over you.
Wisdom is supreme; therefore get wisdom.
    Though it cost all you have, get understanding.
Esteem her, and she will exalt you;
    embrace her, and she will honor you." (Proverbs 4:4–8)

My son, pay attention to what I say;
    listen closely to my words.
Do not let them out of your sight,
    keep them within your heart;
for they are life to those who find them
    and health to a man's whole body. (Proverbs 4:20–22)

Listen and you might hear hope, which you may not have heard
for years. Wisdom actually seeks you. Your job is to hear the voice of
wisdom and learn to love it.

The Source of Wisdom. As you can already tell, wisdom isn't a
system of steps to memorize. Wisdom is quite personal. It comes from
God; it is his voice. You already knew that, but it still might surprise
you. Perhaps you thought God was peeved and waiting for you to finally
get it right; *then* he *might* grace you with his presence. Or maybe *you*
were peeved at God and waiting for *him* to finally get it right. Or both.

Which one? Let the group respond.

In any case, you probably aren't accustomed to thinking of God as the One who goes out into the most dangerous streets, in the middle of the night, searching for you and calling out your name.

> Your friends might never have had *anyone* fight for them. They might not be able to imagine that anyone, including yourself, ever would. If they are awake, this should surprise them.

Perhaps you didn't know that when you veer off into your addiction, he ratchets up his persuasive appeal a few notches.

TWO KINGDOMS

God is the voice of wisdom. He invites you to his kingdom. Your relationship with him is an uneasy and strained one, so it will take some work.

> *Wisdom, folly, kingdoms*—these are not everyday words, but try to stay with them. They are bridges between addiction and the truths of Scripture.

That other voice? Listen to how familiar it sounds. The cartoons have it partly correct: the voice of your addiction really is your own Mini-Me. That's *your* voice you're hearing. Yes, other voices join in, but it is, at least, your own voice. How else would it know you so well? How else would it know exactly how to entice you?

It is the voice of your desires.

The map is now in front of you. The path you are on always comes to a crossroads. One path leads to folly and death, the other to wisdom and life. Study the map, and you will notice that you are actually walking toward a kingdom. You are traveling either toward the kingdom where God is your King and Father, or you are committed to a rival kingdom in which you try to manage life on your own, apart from God. In other words, these decisions are about allegiances. Addiction is the battleground where your loyalties are revealed.

Here is where addicts have an advantage over most people. Addicts know the deeper reality that life is set up according to kingdoms. Addicts know that there isn't one square inch of neutral territory. Everyone is on the way to one kingdom or the other. This may sound like religious gobbledygook to many people, but you know different, even if you aren't sure what you believe about God. You know from your own experience that this is reality. You know all about the crossroads: you have lived with the Mini-Mes battling for your soul on either shoulder. You know that your addiction is a matter of loyalty, of decisions for God or against him. You even know that the central question—not just in addiction but in all of life—is, *Who will I worship? Who will I bow to?* After all, that's what you do with exalted kings.

Some bow to God. If they do, they can't take any credit for it. God pursued them first, in the same way he is pursuing you. Others worship themselves and their own desires through the pursuit of money, security, comfort, prestige, power, drugs, or sex. What distinguishes you from most other false worshipers is that you have chosen to worship something illegal, something more dangerous, or something that carries a higher possibility of bad consequences.

? How do you feel about being identified as a false worshiper? Do you believe it? Do you believe that your life is ultimately about kingdom allegiances?

> These truths might not resonate with your friend or group members just yet. If not, try to understand why, but remember, there is no reason to debate. At this point, just let them continue to receive more light.

TAKE ACTION

The stakes are high. Listen carefully. Two different voices call out to you. It may not feel like it, but you still have the capacity to hear the voice of God who wants to guide you into wisdom and life. You will find that God speaks plainly, not in code. To hear God, you don't need any special skills. You just have to listen to him.

Do something. Listening and action go together. If you are ready to listen, you are ready to act. If you are *not* ready to act, you are not ready to listen.

> When God listens to his people, he does something. He acts. You might want to point out this truth as a way to establish the connection between the Lord and your friend.

Do not merely listen to the word, and so deceive yourselves. Do what it says. Anyone who listens to the word but does not do what it says is like a man who looks at his face in a mirror and, after looking at himself, goes away and immediately forgets what he looks like. But the man who looks intently into the perfect law [God's words] that gives freedom, and continues to do this, not forgetting what he has heard, but *doing* it—he will be blessed in what he does. (James 1:22–25)

? How would you explain this piece of wisdom?

Are you ready to act? The next step will address more about this. But when it comes to addiction, the strategy is to act NOW. Take a step.

Addictions generate a lot of momentum. To act against them seems like a superhuman task. As a matter of fact, it *is* a superhuman task; and you aren't feeling as if you have any superpowers. You're in a rut. You instinctively follow your desires wherever they lead you. You don't question, don't think, and don't resist. But no matter how dead and powerless you feel, at least you are *not* dead. That's good. Change will not be easy. It won't seem natural at first, and you will be sorely tempted to give up after an hour or two. But that resistance is part of the process of becoming a real human being.

You need to do *something*. Keep a pen handy. Write all over this book—in the margins, in the blank spaces. Go ahead and cover it with graffiti. Argue, write down questions, state your disagreements, and jot down ideas on how to put up a fight against temptations. You have been lulled to sleep by Folly. It is time to wake up (Ephesians 5:14)!

Are you awake yet?

How can you tell?

Here are some ways you can take action.

Talk to God. Start by asking for help. Admit it now to God. Simply say, "I need help."

> It sounds easy, but we can only pray because the Spirit empowers us. If any of your friends respond with prayer, remind them that they are not acting like mere humans, but they are acting like children of God. One of your jobs is to point out the movement of the Spirit.

Have you said it?

You may have heard that your problems are usually rooted in your selfishness and pride. Wisdom comes when we take steps of humility. Humility acknowledges a need for help.

Being humbled is not the same thing as being shamed or embarrassed. Being humbled means that you are getting the knack of being human the way God intended. The addict's motto is, "My will, my way." The more human alternative is, "Your will, God. I need help and I am listening."

Talk to another person. You should talk to another person for two reasons: First, by talking about what you have just heard, you will know if you really heard anything. Second, you may need some practice asking for help. If you ask God for help, it should be easy to ask a mere human like yourself for help.

? Who can you talk to?

? What will you ask?

⮕ Your friends are already speaking with you. So once again you can remind them that there is nothing ordinary about this action step. It is evidence that God is on the move. Tell them that. Of course, they can also talk to another person.

Read. If you want more background on the two voices and the two kingdoms, read the first nine chapters of the Book of Proverbs, which is found in the Old Testament of the Bible. You could also read its New Testament counterpart, the Book of James. Then tell someone about what you read.

? Will you begin to read it? Who will you discuss it with?

You probably have all kinds of true and false ideas about the Bible—everyone comes to the Bible with lots of assumptions. Regardless of what you believe, the Bible will be your map, compass, guide, eyes and ears, comfort, defense, ammunition, and even your food.

One reason people avoid the Bible is that it makes them feel guilty, and most people feel they have enough of that already. It is much more helpful to think of the Bible as a light in the darkness. In the darkness you can do forbidden things and believe that nobody sees. That feels like freedom at first, but eventually darkness comes to feel like an isolated prison. Light is always good. It might make you squint. It might make you feel exposed. But it is always good.

Your interest in the Bible will be a gauge. It will measure your desire for change.

> Another reason people avoid Scripture is that it seems ancient and hard to understand. The passages mentioned here are immensely practical, which make them easier to engage. But you are taking small steps toward reading the most important sections of Scripture—the stories of Jesus in the New Testament. Scripture is very personal. It is not a series of self-help steps; it is God's autobiography.

Run. Since the crossroads you face is about life and death, here is some sound advice: RUN. Run like a maniac. Run away. Run from death and everything that it touches.

> The farther we are from the addictive object, the better we are able to hear truth. Addictions are loud. Get close to them, and you can't hear anything else. If you are leading a larger group, suggest that some members might still be deaf to the truth because the object of their addiction is so close and available. You could also ask how many are still walking randomly in the vicinity of their addictive object. Anyone who acknowledges that has just made a step away from his or her addiction.

What would it mean to run from your addiction?

What people or places are contaminated by your addiction?

How will you run from those people and those places? Don't forget, if you get near them, they pull you toward death.

Change your phone number.

Have all the computer sites you hit sent to someone else.

Throw out your secret stash.

? Who will you tell of your plan?

Even if you aren't yet sure what you are running toward—even if you don't know where the safe haven is—you still have to run.

Be afraid. It is best to go into this with a little bit of fear. After all, life and death are being set before you. But don't just fear your addiction. Have a bigger fear. Be afraid of YOU.

> You are tuned to folly's frequency. You are programmed to hear the lies and believe them.
>
> Though you can see the disaster of addiction when you are away from it, as soon as you get close, it starts to look good again.
>
> You think you can manage life on your own.
>
> Though independence is impossible, you prefer the myth of independence to living under the God who created you.

? What are some reasons why you should be afraid of YOU?

Welcome to the path of wisdom and hope. It is honest and clear. You have good reasons to look forward to traveling on it.

> Do you love your friends? Have you decided together on how you can pray for them? In other words, have they been able to ask for prayer, and have you been able to take those requests and anchor them to particular promises of God?
>
> Are those who need extra help getting paired with someone who has practiced running from addiction?

Confess That You Are Double-Minded

MAIN IDEA: Observe your actions. They might reveal that you don't always *want* to change. You do your addiction because you like it. Maybe you want to change, but at the same time, you don't want to change. You are caught between wanting to *trust* God and wanting to *be* God. Acknowledge this, and you are walking in the right direction.

You are probably familiar with Twelve-Step programs. They begin with an acknowledgment of defeat: "We admitted we were powerless over alcohol—that our lives had become unmanageable."*

Yet things are more complicated than that. A weird tension is in your heart. On one side, you feel powerless. Your world feels out of control, and you are sick of it. On the other side, you think that your addiction helps you manage your life so you have *more* control. That's why you hate it *and* you love it. You hate it and you *need* it. Your addiction is not the friend it once was because it has messed up your life. But think about it: you started it because you liked it. It did something for you. Who wants to give up something that works for them?

> Addicts feel as though they are controlled by something else, and
> they are. Here again they are being gently introduced to the idea
> that addictions are not passive or inanimate (or abstract), but they
> actively pursue the addict. Without this, the freedom offered by the
> gospel will sound shallow and secondary.

Do you ever feel like you are in a tug-of-war?

Now add your fear that working through this book is only another opportunity to fail. Why make the effort when there is a risk that you will end up feeling even more like a failure? Better to give up now before you make the investment.

What a mess. No, it's more than that. What you have is a full-blown war! The crossroads at which you stand is not on a quaint country road. It is in a combat zone. One side wants everything to stay the same; the other wants change. One side wants death; the other wants life. One side wants to play God; the other wants to follow God. Your complicated heart can want it both ways, and it is tough to win any battles when you are playing both sides. Then the stalemate becomes an excuse to be hopeless and quit the fight altogether.

---

* *Alcoholics Anonymous* (New York: Alcoholics Anonymous World Services, Inc., 1976).

Quit the fight, and the addiction wins.

Ever been there?

Here is a question to ask yourself: Do you want to change? It is a tougher question than you think.

How can you tell if you *don't* want to change? First, if you are being honest with yourself, you already know it. Second, pay more attention to what you *do* than what you say. Even watch your imaginations—if you say you want to change but notice that you keep going back to your addiction, savoring it in your imagination or hiding and lying, your actions will show what you really love.

If a man says he loves his wife but pursues other women, he doesn't love his wife. His behavior tells the real story. A woman says she loves her husband but indulges in fantasies of being married to other men. Her imaginations tell the real story.

Do you see the deeper reality here? When you want to change and don't want to change, the truth is you don't want to change. When you want both your spouse and someone else, you are rejecting your spouse.

You are very familiar with cravings. These cravings are more than physical desires; they also reveal what you desperately want. Who wants to give up something he or she craves? Your cravings have more of *you* in them than you realize.

> Do you see the repackaging of **cravings**? In the common language of addictions, cravings are strictly biological. Scripture allows you to see even more. Cravings are both biological **and** spiritual.

So start by taking a look at your resistance to change. Honesty and openness are the way of hope.

? Do you want to change? (Circle all that apply to you. Then add your own.)

> You are still trying to create a culture where honesty is prized. These lists give permission to say difficult things.

No, end of story. Does *anybody* really want to change?

No, because that means that somebody else wins. I can already hear the *I-told-you-so's*.

Yes, but I know myself well enough to realize that when someone gives me a law—"Don't use; don't indulge"—I suddenly have a strong urge to break that law.

Yes, but only when I don't have strong cravings.

Yes, but I don't know what I am going to do with the bad feelings.

Yes, but only because I am *supposed* to want to change.

Yes, but not if I really have to say good-bye to something that has become the center of my life. I want the right to visit occasionally.

Yes, but tomorrow, after I can say a fitting good-bye.

Yes, but only because I am embarrassed that I got caught; subtract the embarrassment and I don't see the need.

What other reasons do you have?

? *Why* don't you want to change?

I don't like to be told what I can and can't do.
I hate what I do, but I also love it.
I don't want to try and fail again.
I don't need to change.
My addiction has become like home for me—a comfortable routine.
No one likes to change.

What other reasons do you have?

? Now consider the opposite question: Why *do* you want to change?

For my kids
For my wife
For myself
To restore my relationship with God
Because I am tired of the bad consequences
I don't know

That last question might seem out of place. Why worry about your reasons for changing? When you are desperate, any reason will do.

That's true, but here is why it's worth considering. While some of these reasons might work for a short time, they tend to fade away when cravings are strong. At those times you simply aren't thinking about your family or friends. You just feel like you need your addiction. That's why you need a more powerful motivation to change.

The more powerful reason, of course, is God. He is the King who tells us how to live. But forget about "ought" and "should" for a minute. You have plenty of practice avoiding what God says you ought to do and should do. The real reason God can deliver you is because he is the only one who is more beautiful than your addiction. So not only does he give you power and a reason to say no to your addiction; he also gives you a reason to say yes to something better, something more beautiful and life-giving.

Addictions complicate everything, including your relationship with God. If you are unsure about change, then you are double-minded about God. You know you need him, but you don't necessarily want him—at least not on his terms, which is total surrender. You might feel like he abandoned you in the past, so why would you suddenly switch to his side? To put it crassly, what has he done for you lately?

> Again, this section is encouraging honesty while also helping your friends find words for their ambivalence.

How are you double-minded?

Walk carefully through this one. When you avoid God—and you have—you should be suspicious of your reasons for it. For example, you might notice a hint of anger toward him. Anger often feels absolutely sure of itself. Your attitude can look a little like finger-pointing. Pointing fingers at others and shifting blame is an old trick. Addicts can feel utterly miserable and ashamed but still point the finger at others. Other people aren't usually the real problem.

> This paragraph is action-packed. You might want to pause and see how it speaks on behalf of your friends. If they respond that, yes, they are angry with God, you have taken an important step: you have

identified critical matters of the heart. Other steps will address these issues later. You don't have to say everything at once.

So at least consider the possibility that God isn't the problem.

You might already think that this is too much God-talk. That's fine. Are you a skeptic? A doubter? That is not a problem. Just walk with humility, and be open at this point.

> Since your group members know that you are "religious," they might feel less free to talk about their spiritual doubts. These questions help them voice their concerns about your method or the style of this book.

Remember, you believe all kinds of myths about God. You have stereotyped him; and when you stereotype someone, you don't really know that person. You *think* you do, but only when you actually meet the person and have an actual conversation do you begin to know him accurately.

Since you have been running from God, there is a good chance that you don't really know him.

? Start with a word association test. What words or images come to mind when you think about God?

> Can your group members state how their addiction is about God yet? If they can't, this exercise will seem like busy work. Just move on, and let this book come at the problem from other angles.

Where did you get these ideas?

Here is what God says about himself. This is a favorite way he sets himself apart from all other gods.

The LORD, the LORD, the compassionate and gracious God, slow to anger, abounding in love and faithfulness, maintaining love to thousands, and forgiving wickedness, rebellion and sin.

(Exodus 34:6–7)

Is this what came to your mind when you thought about God?

Here is another way he introduces himself.

"I live in a high and holy place,
    but also with him who is contrite and lowly in spirit,
    to revive the spirit of the lowly
    and to revive the heart of the contrite." (Isaiah 57:15)

What god would ever pursue lowly outcasts? Only *The* God.

Did you notice the words *lowly* and *contrite*? If God really does come close to the humble and hurting, he must understand what life is like for you. This is especially important because only someone who really understands can help you.

> There can be arrogance in addiction, but there is also shame and feeling laid low. If your friends are awake, they should hear God speaking directly to them in their "lowliness"—and they should be surprised.

Lest you feel alone in your internal battle, consider what the apostle Paul had to say about his struggles:

> I have the desire to do what is good, but I cannot carry it out. For what I do is not the good I want to do; no, the evil I do not want to do—this I keep on doing. Now if I do what I do not want to do, it is no longer I who do it, but it is sin living in me that does it. So I find this law at work: When I want to do good, evil is right there with me. For in my inner being I delight in God's law; but I see another law at work in the members of my body, waging war against the law of my mind and making me a prisoner of the law of sin at work within my members.
>
> (Romans 7:18–23)

Who would have thought that you find this in the Bible? You might not always delight in God's law, as Paul wrote, but you certainly can relate to the powerlessness: "What I do is not the good I want to do." God understands how and why you are stuck. That is why you need him.

While we're on the topic of God, it's time to attack the myth that you are too bad to be loved by God or to be forgiven for what you have done. God knows you in detail. Nothing you have done or thought is new to him. Here is the apostle Paul again:

Here is a trustworthy saying that deserves full acceptance: Christ Jesus came into the world to save sinners—of whom I am the worst. But for that very reason I was shown mercy so that in me, the worst of sinners, Christ Jesus might display his unlimited patience as an example for those who would believe on him and receive eternal life. Now to the King eternal, immortal, invisible, the only God, be honor and glory for ever and ever. Amen.

(1 Timothy 1:15–17)

> Take your time. Let your friends establish the pace. This step could easily last more than one meeting.

If anyone is too bad for God's grace, Paul says, he is the one. But God's patience is not like that of an ordinary person. His patience is such that all Paul can do in response is break out into a prayer of thanks and praise.

TAKE ACTION

A wise person does something with all this. Here is what you can do.

> In the following action steps there is no specific encouragement to threaten dealers, pull computer plugs, or put all your money into a custodial account so you can't spend it. Those may be useful steps, but they won't last if they miss the step that is most important: all change goes through the knowledge of God.

Be surprised. If you respond to God with a ho-hum shrug, that's an indication that you might not be getting it. God's grace is astonishing! Shocking! Earth-shattering! In the Bible, those who caught a glimpse of him fell down on their knees and worshiped (Isaiah 6). Even though they knew him, they were still overwhelmed by his greatness, holiness, and beauty. So review the passages mentioned above. Think about them. Let yourself be amazed.

You can learn amazement. You just have to realize that every time you learn about God, you learn about someone who is not ordinary.

> You are especially targeting the beauty and goodness of God here. He doesn't treat us as we deserve, and he runs after wayward children. Behind addictions is the conviction that God isn't good—or not as

good as the addictive object. You are always on the lookout for opportunities to correct that lie.

? Are you bored with this talk about God?

What could keep you from being surprised and amazed?

Be afraid. You have more warrior potential than you think. If real war came to your town and bloodthirsty enemies were at your door, you might be surprised at how fierce you could become. If you had some lead time, you would be looking online to get your hands on an Uzi, grenade launcher, and bazooka. You can get tough if you have to: you need only the proper incentive.

> "From the days of John the Baptist until now, the kingdom of heaven has been forcefully advancing, and forceful men lay hold of it." (Matthew 11:12)

No mercy. The Kingdom of God is not for wimps but for the forceful. But don't be cocky or self-confident. Courage and fear can and should go together. Ask soldiers if they are ever afraid in the face of the enemy. Only a fool is unafraid in the midst of guerilla warfare. Your addiction is in cahoots with the formidable triumvirate of the world, your desires, and the devil. These are not to be trifled with. They should provoke fear.

Fear can control and paralyze. That is not the fear that you aspire to. Your fear is simply an acknowledgment that there is great danger.

> When I am afraid,
>   I will trust in you. (Psalm 56:3)

The problem is not that we can be afraid. The problem is where we turn when we are afraid.

? Are you afraid?

> It takes time to be afraid of sin. At this point, your friends may not have the gift of fear yet—but they can get it.

How can you grow in a good kind of fear?

Hope is in all of this. If you were a zombie or a slave, there would be no point in telling you to fear an enemy and get ruthless. If you are hearing this, you are more alive than you think. You are stronger than you think. Only people with life and vigor are willing to go into battle.

Run. When the fight is lopsided against you—when you are in enemy territory and have strayed from your troop—it is wise to run for safety. That's not weakness; that's just good common sense.

? Where is the danger in your life?

How are you running away from it?

> Yes, this is a question that you read before. There is not a magical key that unlocks the mysteries of addiction. God's path is available to all and clear even to children. The challenge is to REMEMBER. So expect repetition.

Hope. One goal of this step is to acknowledge that you are double-minded. You prefer to linger with old enemies rather than run from them. So if, indeed, you are double-minded, admit the truth. It is only a small step, but it is an important one. In fact, it is a very hopeful one.

? Can you see why acknowledging unattractive things about yourself is hopeful?

Can you identify other reasons to have hope?

Learn more about the Lord. There is no better time than now to know God better. The Scripture, of course, is where you will learn about him and hear his voice. Consider passages like Jeremiah 29:11–14 or Isaiah 40:9–31. As a way to keep focused, write what you find hopeful and helpful in Scripture.

If you are reading other parts of Scripture, look especially for how the passage tells you about God.

> It is natural to bring questions to Scripture. The most important one is, "Lord, who are you?"

Pray. The God of the universe has invited you into a conversation. He speaks first and last, but in the middle he asks you to speak to him.

Yes, it can seem hard to speak to God, but that doesn't mean you are on the wrong path—even the disciples asked Jesus to teach them how to pray. Don't let the challenge stop you.

Prayer is many things—thanks, praise, worship, and requests. In its most basic form, it is simply saying, "Help."

You will find that prayer—communication—is essential to God's way of bringing change in your life. Without it, you might be able to stay away from an addiction, but you won't be transformed. It's like tuning up a broken engine when the real way to fix the car is to give it a total overhaul. New engine. The works.

So don't settle for talking *about* God. Granted, you are feeling a little ashamed because he knows you inside and out. But he knows *everyone* inside and out, and no human life is pretty.

Don't think that he is like a human being. Human beings do not quickly forgive. They don't get overjoyed about taking runaways back; they don't like talking to people who have hated them in the past. But God is not like his creatures. He is holy, and part of what that means is that he genuinely enjoys those who turn humbly to him.

You can speak to God in your own words. If you need help, here is a start:

> Father, I want to talk with you not because I am worthy, but because you are forgiving. Please forgive me for the mess I've made. My heart is divided, and I don't want it to be. I admit that I need help—lots of help. I can't live a wise life—the life I was intended to live as your child—on my own. I need you.

In a group, prayer will take an increasingly important place. It will encourage humility because you are asking for help. It will produce hope because you are going to the One who promises to hear and act.

Are you feeling more awake?

Be sure to ask yourself this question. Isn't it true that we can all fall asleep? How many sermons have you heard? Of those sermons, how many did you really hear? The addict is no different than anyone else. We all need to be roused from our spiritual slumber.

STEP 3:

Know Your Story

MAIN IDEA: Addictions don't simply pounce on unsuspecting victims. They follow a predictable pattern. They start with personal hardships and end with voluntary slavery.

> Our lives are a story that can be told in many different ways.
> "My father left us when I was seven, and I have been trying to numb the pain ever since."
> "Alcoholism runs in my family."
> "Once I was blind, but now I see."
> The goal is to learn how God tells our story. This step will be the first opportunity to learn God's retelling. As people share their stories in your group, don't expect every one to be in perfect harmony with the way God tells it yet. It takes our entire lives to learn the real story.
> For background information you could read chapter 4 of *Addictions—A Banquet in the Grave.*

What happened? How did you get here? One day you were walking around like a normal person and BAM! The next thing you knew, you were flat on your back. An addiction became the center of your universe.

Like most everything else, your addiction started small and gradually grew. What began as a random, casual walk ended in the prison of a dark kingdom. You don't know how you got there, and you fear there is no way out. But you actually took a well-worn path. There is a way out.

The retelling of your story can help you to wake up when you start veering off The Way.

YOUR DESCENT

1. Some addictions begin very simply. You tried something and you liked it. But it is more likely that you first said, **"I don't like the way I feel."**

Addictions temporarily change the way you feel. By doing so, they change your view of yourself and the world. You didn't like the way you felt. Life wasn't working. It may be difficult to remember what life felt like before your addiction. Maybe the thought of returning to that forgotten state scares you. But know this: if you ran to your addictions with your bad feeling and your broken world, your world still feels bad and broken. Only now, you have the shame and guilt and new pains of addiction heaped on your old pains.

? What was so bad about your pre-addiction life? Something was wrong, or you wouldn't have traded that reality for a state of addiction. What were the miseries that drove you in that direction? How was your world becoming unmanageable? How *is* it unmanageable?

> There is a lot of pain in addictions groups. A lot of pain. The long-term goal is for your friends to learn how to stop turning to their addictions and start turning to the Lord in their pain.

Do you know what to do with these things? You can't ignore them. What is your plan? Who can help? Don't forget, God is "the compassionate and gracious God."

> A possible action step here could be to have group members find a Psalm that can guide them to the Lord in the midst of their pain. The problem of pain will be addressed again later.

Hint: You grow in wisdom one small step at a time. Start with only one thing, and take a small step.

2. In response to your misery you said, **"I want to manage my world my way,"** which meant, whether you knew it consciously or not, that you wanted to manage your world apart from God.

It wasn't an audible voice, but you were saying something about God—and you still are. Somewhere in the back of your mind you knew there was God, but you are just like the rest of humanity: you wanted to manage your world yourself. You thought you knew better.

> The word *sin* doesn't always make sense to addicts because they associate sin with highly intentional wrongdoing, and addictions seem automatic. One reason the word *sin* hasn't appeared yet is because the word often carries this misinterpretation. This section introduces how sin can be much less intentional. Indeed, sin is instinctive and natural. We sin even without conscious intent.

You might not have said anything as blatant as, "God, forget it. I am going my own way." But everything in your life is connected to

God. God is your Maker—your Father—and everything you do is either moving toward him and his kingdom or away from him. You were the child who wanted independence and said, "I am going out into the world on my own. I don't want to be accountable to my Father or be under his roof. I want to manage my own life."

In other words, you were acting like a regular human being.

Can you see the connection between your actions and God? Does it make sense?

> When you are angry you are saying, "God isn't good. I deserve better. I want to be God."
>
> When you feel sorry for yourself you are saying, "I deserve better from God."
>
> When you complain you are saying, "I deserve better from God. God isn't good."
>
> When you are afraid you are saying, "God can't be trusted. He is not with me."
>
> When you don't love others you are saying, "God isn't good to me, so I don't have to be good to others. I am going to treat others the way I have been treated."
>
> When you lie you are saying, "I can hide from God."
>
> When you are depressed you are saying, "God doesn't care. I have no hope."

? When you started the descent into your addiction, you were saying something about God. What were you saying?

I want to go my own way, at least in this one area.
You can't be trusted to help.
I want what I want, and I'm not sure you will give it to me.

Anything else?

3. Instead of turning toward God, you turned toward your future addiction and said, **"I like this. This is what I have been looking for."**

Addictions don't just happen. They creep up on you with small steps *you* allow or even initiate. It is as if you see caged lions, inch toward their cage, unlock the door, invite them to come out, and tease them a bit. Then you are mystified when they devour you. You weren't expecting your addiction to enslave you.

? What small steps can you see in hindsight?

4. Since you liked it, you said, **"I want to keep doing this!"**

When you really like something, you do it again. That is what you did with your addiction. You practiced. What you couldn't see was that you were showing early signs of being taken captive. You felt alive—sort of. But the more you practiced your addiction, the less your brain was working. Maybe your arms weren't outstretched like a zombie's, but your eyes were glazed. Maybe the signs were more subtle—the way you used your money or your computer or your free time or the way you talked with your family when they asked about your day. Secretly, more and more of your life was becoming about your addiction. The object of your affection seemed to have a life of its own as it sucked the life out of you. But this, of course, is all in retrospect. You didn't really notice at the time.

? Is there anything you want to note from the early days of practicing your addiction?

5. Over time, your addiction began to serve more and more purposes in your life. You said, **"This means so much to me. I love it."**

As addictions develop, they seem to meet more needs in your life and become more important. For example, what might have started as a way to be accepted evolved into a way to deal with pain, which grew into a way to deal with *any* emotion, which . . . .

? What did your addiction do for you? Why did you love it so much? It is worthwhile to remember because you might still love it more than you realize.

? What emotions did it help you cope with?

For example, "I am angry at _____ because
_____."

"I am afraid of _____, and my addiction eases the fear
and helps me relax."

"I am a failure and I can't face the shame."

Your long-term goal is to learn how God speaks to the purposes
your addiction serves in your life. For example, if one of your goals was
to numb your pain, you will need to learn instead how to turn to God
with your pain. It may take a while, but you can learn.

Your addiction hurt, but it also helped with lots of things—things
like relationships, situations, failures, emotions, fears, pain, and shame.
Do you have any ideas about what God might say to you about those
things? Here is where you need to talk with a wise friend who has
walked with God and can direct you.

> Addictions cause shame, but they also offer relief from shame. It
> might be fruitful here to discuss how God surprises people who his
> experience shame by covering the naked, cleansing the unclean, and
> loving the outcast (e.g., Ps. 34:5, Luke 6:17–19, Luke 8:43–48, 1 Pet.
> 2:9–10). Check to see if your friends have insights about how God
> takes away shame, especially as they have begun to experience the
> early stages of deliverance from their addictions.

By this time in your addiction, you went underground. You practiced in secret, and you probably told some whoppers to cover it up.

6. Anything that becomes the center of your world—other than
   God—is ultimately going to leave you feeling empty. Your addic-
   tion is no different. You said, **"I want more. I NEED more."**
   Meanwhile, it became less satisfying.

> Jeremiah 2:13 comes to mind. "My people have committed two sins:
> They have forsaken me, the spring of living water, and have dug their
> own cisterns, broken cisterns that cannot hold water." A cistern was
> used to collect water in arid climates; you can imagine that the water
> in a cistern wouldn't be nearly as refreshing as spring water.

? Do you see the insanity of addiction? You believed that your addiction would *cure* your emptiness rather than become another *cause*. What do you believe now?

Emptiness is a sign that you were looking for satisfaction in places that were not intended to satisfy human beings. In response, you need to change your diet. You have to identify what is healthy and truly satisfying. You have to retrain your appetite, which will take time. Your desires are attracted to things that can kill you. Now you need to learn what is truly best and develop a taste for it. With this in mind, God says to you, "Taste and see that the LORD is good" (Psalm 34:8).

? What are your ideas for retraining your appetites?

7. Next, you were mastered. You said to your addiction, **"You are my god."**

By this time, your addiction went from being a friend to a lover to a slave-master. The object of your affection, which was once only a line of powder, a bottle, or underwear models in the daily paper, morphed into an idol. It had its own sacred place in your life, and you worshiped it whenever you could. This idol, however, drained the life out of you.

Can you picture it?

Even other people started to notice that you were not the same. You were still doing what you wanted, but you were also a slave.

▷ Be sure your friends see the development. Addiction starts with **voluntary** and ends in **slavery**.

? When did you begin to notice that you were a slave?

8. Once mastered, you experienced bitter tragedy. You said, **"This hurts. I've been betrayed. I want it, but I don't want it."**

When you devote yourself to anything other than the true God, it will eventually betray you. It will make promises, but it won't deliver on them. Gradually, it will corrupt everything around you and hurt both you and other people.

Money, health, relationships, guilt, shame, and on and on—so many things are touched by addiction. It might have felt like it was just about your own private world, but then the dominoes started falling. No doubt some of them fell on other people.

? What have been the most significant consequences of your addiction?

Again, here are the steps that go down to addiction.

> 1. I don't like the way I feel.
>
> 2. I want to manage my world my way.
>
> 3. I like this. This is what I have been looking for.
>
> 4. I want to keep doing this!
>
> 5. This means so much to me. I love it.
>
> 6. I want more. I NEED more.
>
> 7. You are my god.
>
> 8. This hurts. I've been betrayed. I want it, but I don't want it.

You can sum it up this way: addiction is **voluntary slavery**. You want it and pursue it. Meanwhile, it wants you and pursues you. As you learn to interpret what happened to you, try to keep "voluntary" and "slavery" in balance because you need to understand both.

When you understand that your behavior is voluntary, you are more apt to be active and fight against it.
When you understand that you are a slave, you are more apt to call out for help from God and then other people.

By the way, the "slavery" of voluntary slavery is why addiction feels like a disease. Physical dependence may be one part of the slavery.

? When you reflect on your story, what about your addiction has been voluntary? How has it been slavery?

GOD'S RESPONSE

None of this sounds pretty. It's rough even to think about it. After all you have been through, you might feel as though someone is hitting you while you are down. It would be easier on you if you could tell your story of addiction like this: "I was out on an innocent walk, minding my own business and then, without warning, I fell into a deep pit with no way out." Indeed, that is one way to tell the story, but you want the real and deeper story. Real is good. You want the story that can take a more penetrating look at your heart. As you adopt it, you might notice a sting at first, but it is the sting of antiseptic that heals.

For that sting to heal, there is one other crucial part of the story. "Then I turned to God and listened." As you listen, those words should sound good. They should sound like words of *The* God who takes your hand and leads you out of the pit. Otherwise, they are not God's words.

> "I will give thanks to you, O Lord,
> for though you were angry with me,
> your anger turned away,
> that you might comfort me." (Isaiah 12:1, ESV)

Don't be alarmed by that comment about God's anger. Of course the Lord can be angry with us when we rebel against him, but his anger is not like any anger you have ever seen. It always listens to you. It is always patient. It always invites you to return. It is quick to forgive. It always says yes. God says that his anger is restrained and only lasts for a moment; his comfort is boundless and enduring. He is not what you expected. He is the God of "unlimited patience" (1 Timothy 1:16).

TAKE ACTION

Are you awake? You are seeking wisdom, and you need your wits about you. You know you are awake if you take action.

Ask the group members how awake they are feeling, on a scale of 1–10.

Review. Can you summarize what has been said so far? Without looking, what were the first two steps? What was meaningful one day can be forgotten the next, so take some time to review where you have been.

When in doubt, talk less and let the group talk more.

What has been helpful?

What has been confusing?

What have you done?

Run. You are in training to be a marathoner, not a sprinter. There will be lots of dangers to run from.

Where are the dangers?

There it is again. When you are in a war, you stay vigilant. If your friends detect a desire to take a few days off from the battle, they are witnessing their desires in action. They might want to lose to their addiction more than they realize.

Can you identify the accomplices (people, places, moods) of your addiction? You have to run from those too.

Here is a law of addictions: the closer you are to your once-beloved object, the greater your temptation. The farther you are, the less the temptation. So you want to run as far as possible.

Do you see the logic of this principle? While sitting in a group and talking about these matters, it is easy to say no. But put the desired object right in front of you, add a little privacy, and cravings suddenly run amok.

Have hope. This isn't the last time you'll hear this action step. I know what you're thinking: if you could make yourself have hope, you would have done it long ago. But when wisdom creeps in, you can actually choose to have hope.

Have hope because you are listening to wisdom.

Have hope because, if you got yourself into an addiction, there is also a way out.

Have hope because, as unattractive as this descent into addiction is, you are facing reality. You are coming alive. You are moving from the shadows to the light.

Have hope because *The* God who saw your descent is ready, willing, and able to forgive you and give you power to crawl, walk, run, and soar.

"When I am weak, then I am strong" (2 Corinthians 12:10). You don't feel like you have the "strong" part down, but you feel like an expert in "weak." Good. You are halfway there.

Here is a heads-up on what is in store for you. Please don't think that all this is about doing better and trying harder. In some sense it is, but there is much more. The banquet you are aiming for takes place in a new kingdom with a new Lord. Right now it feels like you are giving things up. But in reality you are inheriting a new kingdom. You won't feel shortchanged.

> "Do not be afraid, little flock, for your Father has been pleased to give you the kingdom." (Luke 12:32)

> "The LORD your God is with you,
>   he is mighty to save.
>   He will take great delight in you,
>   he will quiet you with his love,
>   he will rejoice over you with singing." (Zephaniah 3:17)

God will rejoice over you. He is pleased to give you the kingdom. That's hope! Watch out if you are holding onto your hopelessness. Hopelessness authorizes you to ease back into addiction.

? From 1 to 10, where are you on the scale of hope?

10 = certainty that God and his kingdom are promised to you

1 = you can't believe that God would forgive and accept you (or you don't want him to)

1	2	3	4	5	6	7	8	9	10

Hopelessness   Hope

If you are below 5, be sure to talk with someone.

> Always be looking for evidences of spiritual life. If your friends have
> made it this far, that in itself is reason to be encouraged. No doubt
> there are other evidences of life too. Tell your friends when you see
> good things.

Confess. The more you see the real story, the more you will want to confess your wrong to the Lord. That's what happens in relationships.

When in doubt, confess how you voluntarily strayed from him. Such confession nurtures humility and brings more reality into your once hazy condition.

> Contrary to popular belief, confession is not self-flagellation. It is a
> way of coming into the light. It is a door to God's wonderful reality.
> When friends begin to confess specific features of their addiction to
> the Lord, you can be sure that the Spirit is on the move in their lives.
> Be sure to point it out.

It might still be awkward for you to talk to God. It is a new relationship, and you aren't accustomed to talking to him. You might still feel guilty for what you have done (or are doing). Perhaps you think you might go back to your addiction, and it seems a bit phony to speak with him when you aren't sure if you want him to intrude. It's fine to tell God that too.

But don't wait to speak to him. Be honest when you do. If you want to read some prayers to God, get a Bible and open to Psalms 6, 10, 13, 14, 25, or 73. You will find gut-level honesty on every page.

Start talking to him.

Lord, my natural tendency is to go my own way. I am sorry,
yet I still feel the same old tug. Forgive me. Help me.

Retell your story. One way to nurture hope is to get in sync with God's interpretation of reality. You already began doing this when you came to see that the skirmish you are fighting with your addiction is part of a much larger battle for kingdom allegiances. This step goes deeper. It shows how, beneath addictive behaviors, there are desires that gradually rule you. You have to learn to fear them and fight them. If you want a vivid and true picture of them, envision yourself bowing down to an idol. That's what addiction is: a false god. You have been its worshiper.

When you retell your story, be sure to include the part about God's patience with you. The more you know about God, the more you will change. And, of course, you don't want to abuse his patience.

> Do you show contempt for the riches of his kindness, toler-
> ance and patience, not realizing that God's kindness leads
> you toward repentance? (Romans 2:4)

? Can you retell your personal story in this new way? Have you actually told it to someone?

> When group members learn how to tell their stories more accurately,
> you will notice that they are well on their way to the kingdom of God.
> They are hearing God's voice and following him. So what sounds like a
> simple telling of a story is actually a profound way to wage the battle
> at the crossroads.

Go Public

MAIN IDEA: Be open and honest. Addictions are like mushrooms that thrive in the darkness. That is where addictions can feed on lies. A further step toward change is to bring them into the open and speak the truth.

> When it comes to going public, addicts report that they can open up in AA and its affiliates more easily than they can with people in the church. There can be a number of reasons for this that span from an addict's hard-heartedness to a church's condemnation and self-righteous judgment. Whatever the reason, a church wants to do what it can to create a place where people can speak freely for the purpose of learning God's ways. Public honesty is a potent way to say no to Satan's kingdom. Public honesty is evidence that God is bringing his kingdom into the heart of an addict. In other words, no matter how sad the stories group members reveal, you have reasons to encourage them that God is drawing them to himself. He is giving them strength in the battle even as they are honestly sharing their stories. An addiction is nothing to cheer about, but even the smallest step of honesty is reason to celebrate.
>
> This step comes at a time when your friends are beginning to trust you. Perhaps they will bring more secrets into the light. If they do, be blessed and encourage them.
>
> For background reading, consider chapter 9 of **Addictions— A Banquet in the Grave**.

God intended us to live our lives openly. No masks. No cover-ups. No lies. Before sin complicated everything, Adam and Eve were "naked and unashamed." Imagine how great it would be if we could make a return visit.

It's no surprise, then, that wisdom—knowing how to live life the way God intended—lives out in the open, without secrets or back-room dealings. It walks in the light rather than the darkness.

Have you been exposed? Have you ever been caught in your addiction? It was horrible, no doubt, but that experience gives you another opportunity to revise your story. Being exposed was embarrassing, yet here is the reality: God loves you too much to let you persist in darkness. The worst thing imaginable is for you to be free to go down your dark, addictive path. The best thing is for God to intrude, shine his light, and lead you in a new direction. People who really love you try to intervene when they see you on a path that will kill you. When you get caught, it is a reason to thank God.

> The path of the righteous is like the first gleam of dawn,
>   shining ever brighter till the full light of day.
> But the way of the wicked is like deep darkness;
>   they do not know what makes them stumble.
>
> (Proverbs 4:18–19)

> You have set our iniquities before you,
>   our secret sins in the light of your presence.
>
> (Psalm 90:8)

Are you on board? Does getting exposed sound good?

Is there anything in your life that you refuse to take public? That doesn't mean you have to go public with everything. That would be a full-time job. It *does* mean that you would be *willing* to go public with anything, and you *have* gone public with things you would have preferred to keep in the closet.

? What are you ashamed of and unwilling to speak about to anyone?

What are you still hiding?

Picture it this way: Imagine your life as a movie that has access to your thoughts and behaviors. What would embarrass you when the movie went on the Internet?

? How do you feel about this step? Do you see its benefit?

? What guidelines do you have for revealing a secret addiction? When should you confess lies to another person? To whom should you confess? If your addiction has lasted a long time, you have told so many lies to so many people that it would be impossible to confess to every person. If you won't be able to confess to everyone, how do you decide whom to speak to, and what will you say?

These are difficult decisions. You will need help. So now is an ideal time to go public. At least you can go public with someone who might have wisdom on these matters.

A rule of thumb: when in doubt, it is usually wiser to err on the side of speaking more openly.

Another rule of thumb: if you are going public with someone you have hurt, get advice on how to do it. You might end up feeling a little better—confession is, indeed, good for the soul—but other people might feel blasted at point-blank range. More on this will come in a later step.

TRUTH AND LIES

What we are talking about is truth and lies. Lies cover up. They maintain their private strategies even as they make everything much worse. Truth has nothing to hide. It is open and honest.

When you try to hide in darkness, a lot of your lies don't get noticed—not at first, anyway. Other people don't detect them; you might not even see them yourself. When lies become your native language, you are in trouble. Just as a person's language reveals his country of origin, so lies show your allegiances.

Lies reveal allegiances. Here is more reality. When you try to manage your world apart from God, your allegiances are to yourself and your own kingdom. You know that, but there is more. You are actually part of an alliance. Satan himself is behind this turf war. When you speak lies, you are speaking the language of *his* faltering but very real kingdom. This is why you can be enslaved in the kingdom of your own making. Any kingdom where God is not King has Satan as its lord.

> [Jesus said,] "Why is my language not clear to you? Because you are unable to hear what I say. You belong to your father, the devil, and you want to carry out your father's desire. He was a murderer from the beginning, not holding to the truth, for there is no truth in him. When he lies, he speaks his native language, for he is a liar and the father of lies. Yet because I tell the truth, you do not believe me!" (John 8:43–45)

Do you notice how when you listen to God it is like turning on the lights? It might not be pretty at first, with all the cockroaches skittering toward the corners. Not everything you see will comfort you, but the more you see the better prepared you will be.

? What do you think about the alliance between your addictive object, your desires, and Satan himself? Does it make sense to you? Do you believe that it really happens?

⇨ Use your judgment if your friends are not making the connection between the addictive object, their own desires, and Satan himself. The basic point is that life is lived in a kingdom. If they grasp the bigger picture but not the details, that is enough for now.

A lie is more than a lie. You did something wrong, and you want to hide it. That is understandable. But there is more to it than that. When you lie, you are declaring your loyalties. You are imitating the wrong lord. You are speaking Satan's native language!

⇨ It is amazing how Scripture allows us to see everything with more depth and light.

In contrast, God has revealed the Way and the Truth. Jesus is God in the flesh. He said, "I am the way and the truth and the life" (John 14:6). "It is impossible for God to lie" (Hebrews 6:18). Watch Jesus and you will hear him say, "Verily, verily." (You will find it one hundred times in the New Testament.) This means, "Truly, truly." By it Jesus shows the difference between himself and all false teachers.

Yes, this is a huge deal. You can't have a relationship unless you and the other person speak the truth. You can't have a relationship unless you speak the same language. Even more, when you are part of a kingdom, you imitate its king.

Here is another rule of life: Speak the truth and you imitate Jesus. Speak lies and you imitate Satan.

? You were intended to speak the truth. That is how you were created. What would it look like to speak the truth? How would it be liberating?

⇨ You want the group to see that God's wisdom makes sense. It really is the better way.

It's time to get suspicious. Our tendency is to be suspicious of others because we are afraid they will uncover us, but our suspicion is best directed toward ourselves. Take a step toward the light. Search for the lies you tell. They come in many different forms.

White lies
Whoppers
Defensiveness
Hiding
Sneaking
Blaming
Justifying
Giving your word and not keeping it

Through lies you attempt to fool others, but you are fooling yourself. The devil is a schemer. When you are lured in his direction, you speak his language and you believe his lies. You are another victim in a long line that goes back to the beginning of history.

You could say that human history turned at the point when Adam and Eve believed Satan's lies and doubted the truthfulness and generosity of God. This continues to be the turning point of your life too. Satan minimizes wrong behavior—a lie that is intended to kill you—and he promises you a kingdom—a lie that fails to disclose the fine print.

> Now the serpent was more crafty than any of the wild animals the LORD God had made. He said to the woman, "Did God really say, 'You must not eat from any tree in the garden'?"
>
> The woman said to the serpent, "We may eat fruit from the trees in the garden, but God did say, 'You must not eat fruit from the tree that is in the middle of the garden, and you must not touch it, or you will die.'"
>
> "You will not surely die," the serpent said to the woman. "For God knows that when you eat of it your eyes will be opened, and you will be like God, knowing good and evil."
>
> (Genesis 3:1–5)

These lies are subtle and familiar. They are echoed in your life every day. They are lies about God and about you.

"God doesn't care about me."

"God doesn't care about one drink (binge, look, hit . . .). It's not like I am killing anyone."

"God is about love and forgiveness, so he will understand."

What other lies about God do you believe?

God is not good. He is holding out on me.

God could never love someone like me.

God could never forgive someone like me. (Pay attention to this one. If you doubt forgiveness of sins, you are setting yourself up for a fall. Your argument will be that God has forsaken you, so why bother trying anymore?)

God doesn't see.

God wouldn't want me to abandon my friends.

Any others?

? When you speak and believe lies, you are a voluntary slave. Satan victimizes you, but you also want to believe lies. What's the payoff? Why would you want to believe lies?

Is the map in view? When you blindly follow your desires, you are making a beeline for the dark kingdom. A kingdom has a particular culture, a way of doing things. The kingdom of darkness operates in the shadows, and all transactions are made with lies. When lies become natural to you, you can tell when you are in the dark kingdom. But, even more diabolic is that you believe lies.

Are you able to discern the voice of truth, which calls you to The Way? What does it sound like?

> When you walk with addicts, you will be lied to. It goes with the territory. But don't take those lies personally (though they are, indeed, personal). Liars believe lies, and they are in bondage to the father of lies. That is reason for grief and compassion, not anger.

TAKE ACTION

This step could keep you busy for a while. The longer you indulged your addiction, the more lies you told and the more lies you believed. The good news is that you don't have to make a perfect and exhaustive review of your lies before you head toward God's kingdom. In fact, if *anything* in this step makes sense and makes truth-telling sound more attractive to you, that's evidence that you are already turning to the true kingdom.

Go public. If you haven't spoken publicly about your addiction to anyone, now is the time to do it. It could be a pastor, a wise friend, or a person who is farther down the path of truth in their own battle with addictions. If you have spoken publicly, then consider what you are presently hiding. It is easy to give out sound bites of truth to other people in order to keep them from asking about anything else. In other words, you tell a small truth in order to cover up a big lie. When in doubt, be more open rather than less. If your openness might deeply hurt someone you love, get advice from someone else to decide how to say the truth and when.

Confess to God. Anytime now, you should look forward to confession to God. It should feel like a cool shower after working all day in 100-degree heat. Confess that you have spoken the wrong language. Confess that you have *purposefully* believed lies because they gave you the independence you wanted. Confess your helplessness to leave the darkness and lies apart from his power. Confess that you are still full of faults that are hidden even from you (Psalm 19:12).

What is amazing about this confession is that you don't have to confess perfectly to be okay before God. You don't have to search endlessly for those hard-to-find lies and deeper motives. You are accepted by God simply because he accepts you, not because you are a great confessor. Perfection is not your goal; trust is. When your aim is perfection, you are actually headed away from God because you are trusting in your own acts rather than trusting God. You should be finding God to be quite trustworthy.

⇨ It is simple: We confess; God forgives (1 John 1:9). In fact, he delights in those who turn from their sins.

Then Jesus told them this parable: "Suppose one of you has a hundred sheep and loses one of them. Does he not leave the ninety-nine in the open country and go after the lost sheep until he finds it? And when he finds it, he joyfully puts it on his shoulders and goes home. Then he calls his friends and neighbors together and says, 'Rejoice with me; I have found my lost sheep.' I tell you that in the same way

there will be more rejoicing in heaven over one sinner who
repents than over ninety-nine righteous persons who do
not need to repent." (Luke 15:3–7)
Is anyone interested in delighting God?

Ask God. The Bible is God's communication of truth to you. You
are going to want to read it more often. As you do, it will teach you how
to ask God for what he wants to give you. Here is one example that you
can ask for now:

Search me, O God, and know my heart;
    test me and know my anxious thoughts.
See if there is any offensive way in me,
    and lead me in the way everlasting. (Psalm 139:23–24)

There is no fear in being revealed when you know that God is
pleased by your openness. After all, he *already* knows your heart. When
you confess and ask him to search you, you are turned in his direction.

> Change is a personal matter. You are changed by THE person, the tri-
> une God. And there is nothing more personal than prayer.

Retell your story. This step adds more to your story. The bigger
picture is coming into view: kingdoms, allegiances, truth, lies, imitating
your king, darkness, light. It has all the ingredients. God, in Scripture,
has already told this story. You, in turn, are learning it from him. If it
is all new, listen to others tell their stories. Meanwhile, practice telling
your own. There will be more details to come.

Whom will you tell? As you can guess, an accurate retelling of your
story will bless other people.

Know more about God. God never gets tired of inviting you out of
darkness and into the light. Here is a passage from the New Testament
that talks about how Jesus is the light.

"The people living in darkness have seen a great light; on
those living in the land of the shadow of death a light has
dawned." From that time on Jesus began to preach, "Repent,
for the kingdom of heaven is near." (Matthew 4:16–17)

God draws people to the light as they confess their fault, which is called "repentance" in this passage. Repentance means turning away from darkness and the false kingdom to Jesus and the true kingdom.

There are various ways to show allegiance to your king. You obey him, worship him, and follow him. Perhaps the most common way is that you *trust* the king.

> Then Jesus told them . . . "The man who walks in the dark does not know where he is going. Put your trust in the light while you have it, so that you may become sons of light." (John 12:35–36)

If you trust and follow God, tell him. If you aren't so sure, tell him. Then keep listening to who he is and what he says. Read about Jesus, who is God himself. You will find his history in the Books of Matthew, Mark, Luke, or John. Consider reading Luke 4–8 and notice how Jesus, who is God, is always pursuing the outcasts and the people who were considered unclean. This is One you will want to follow.

Don't just read the stories about him; truly listen. Determine whether or not you think he is trustworthy.

Know *the* God

MAIN IDEA: All change is personal. It is not a matter of knowing techniques, strategies, or to-do lists. It is a matter of knowing a person.

> One task of a small group is to connect our relationship with God to all the details of everyday life. Addictions hide that connection, but you want to emphasize it. You could have one person share his or her story. Ask that person to highlight how this story is about God and himself or herself.
>
> If addictions are all about God, then these next two steps are the very heart of change. You can't change your worship unless you find greater worth in a different object of worship. You can't change allegiances unless the other King is much better than the despot you presently serve.
>
> There is a curious direction to biblical change. We begin by looking at our complicated and dark hearts, but then we look away from ourselves and look to Another. The true knowledge of the glorious God—that's where the action is.
>
> For background reading, consider chapters 7 and 8 from **Addictions—A Banquet in the Grave.**

Feeling awake yet? Are you making decisions? When you face the crossroads—and you do every day—you have to make decisions.

Consider how you have changed during your life—both for the good and for the bad. Change, you will find, usually involves another person.

Your father was abusive.
Your father said an encouraging word just when you needed it.
Your spouse betrayed you.
Your spouse stood beside you during a tough time.
Your neighbor slandered you to other neighbors.
Your neighbor came to you and spoke truth, even though it meant risking the relationship.

Find change points in your life, and you will find people.

This basic principle reflects a deeper reality: the way out of addiction is to know *The* Person. The way out is to know the true God. There is no other path to true change. Other changes might make life a little easier, but you are still trapped in the same dark kingdom. The goal is to know God in such a way that you will find him greater to you than whatever else you love. Along the way, as you get to know God, you will notice that you are more fully human and alive. That is what love does to us.

Here are some of the highlights of who he is.

GOD IS THE CREATOR

"In the beginning God created." Scripture starts with a bang! There is only one God, and he created all things.

Listen to the following questions, asked by God himself. They are rhetorical. You don't have to give answers because the answers are obvious. But, still, the questions can teach you a great deal.

> Who has measured the waters in the hollow of his hand,
>   or with the breadth of his hand marked off the heavens?
> Who has held the dust of the earth in a basket,
>   or weighed the mountains on the scales
>   and the hills in a balance?
> Who has understood the mind of the LORD,
>   or instructed him as his counselor?
> Whom did the LORD consult to enlighten him,
>   and who taught him the right way?
> Who was it that taught him knowledge
>   or showed him the path of understanding?
> Surely the nations are like a drop in a bucket;
>   they are regarded as dust on the scales;
>   he weighs the islands as though they were fine dust.
>   (Isaiah 40:12–15)

 The truth that God is the Creator is more than a rallying cry to do battle with evolutionists. For the Old Testament saints, it was a source of great comfort.

Notice that, as Creator, God speaks with authority to all his creation. He has control over his creation, and he is intimately involved with it. He is close. If you *really* believe that God is close to you and he is the powerful Creator, it makes a difference. What difference does it make?

You belong to God. Whatever you create belongs to you. That means you belong to God. In all your life you have never been in neutral territory. You belong to one kingdom or the other. God is your Creator, and he is on a mission to make you his own again. It is nice to be wanted, isn't it?

Your story is getting even more detail. You were created by God, and you belong to him. Apparently, like everyone else, you were a child who wanted independence.

? What does it mean to really believe that God created all things, including you, and that you belong to him?

Don't worship other gods. Throughout the Bible God emphasizes that he is the Creator. His intent is to have us understand that we belong to him. Therefore, we don't worship other gods because they are not *our* God. But we worship other gods anyway. The Old Testament is the story of God's people worshiping idols, God disciplining them, and God calling them back to himself. The same story continues today.

Go to almost any country in the world and you will find idols—false gods. Among Western nations idol worship is less visible, but the human heart is the same everywhere. If you find idol worship in Bangkok, you will find it in your house too.

What idol do you worship? Your addiction is one idol. It has been the center of your life. It has taken the place that rightly belonged to God. You bow to it, although when you bow to it, your purpose is *not* to be its servant. Your intent is to worship the idol so it will give you what you want. At root, idol worship is about our own desires. We worship an idol because we think it will give us pleasure, security, power, peace, or prosperity. Selfishness, indeed, runs even more deeply than we realize.

Does idolatry fit your story? Can you see that when you rename your addiction as idolatry, you are naturally pointed back to God as the only answer? That's the way you want to tell your story.

You now have the fuller picture of the false kingdom. It is a kingdom where your desires reign, where Satan is the personal lord. That is not to say that people consciously worship Satan. They worship idols, which serve as his proxy. This is the triumvirate that sets itself up against God: the world (with its idols), our own desires, and the devil.

Now get ready to be surprised. Here is a passage in which God directs words of comfort to idolaters—people who have worshiped something in creation instead of him. They have turned away from him and tried to find a world where *they* could be god. Who would have thought that he would offer words of comfort?

> Do you not know?
>> Have you not heard?
> The LORD is the everlasting God,
>> the Creator of the ends of the earth.
> He will not grow tired or weary,
>> and his understanding no one can fathom.
> He gives strength to the weary
>> and increases the power of the weak.
> Even youths grow tired and weary,
>> and young men stumble and fall;
> but those who hope in the LORD
>> will renew their strength.
> They will soar on wings like eagles;
>> they will run and not grow weary,
>> they will walk and not be faint. (Isaiah 40:28–31)

God extends that promise to idolaters! You might not know what it is like to run and fly, but doesn't this give you hope? Doesn't it make you feel more alive? Something is up ahead for you, and it is good. You are worse than you think, but that is no reason to run and hide—we all are worse than we think. The good news is that only the Spirit of God can reveal such things. So if that is what you believe, you can be encouraged that God loves you and is beginning to purge you of your idols. This means that God is *better* than you think. You keep waiting for the axe to fall, but instead you receive patience and mercy.

When you are hearing good and true things, you don't want to go too long without talking to the Lord.

> God, I don't feel like I can even crawl. I don't even feel human sometimes. But I hear you. Somehow you renew the strength of weak people like me. Will you please renew my strength?

? Anything else you want to say to him?

He created you for a reason. When you create something, you have a purpose in mind. You do it for a reason.

> "Bring my sons from afar
>> and my daughters from the ends of the earth—
> everyone who is called by my name,
>> *whom I created for my glory*,
>> whom I formed and made." (Isaiah 43:6–7, emphasis added)

As you have heard people say, it is not about you. God created you for *his* glory. When something is glorious, it is spectacular, brilliant—it is irresistible and beautiful. If you want to be a true human being, set out to advertise to the world that God is glorious. In other words, your job is to make him famous. An amazing job description, isn't it? You have the job of royal ambassador if you are willing to take it.

? Any ideas about what that means? What would it look like to be an ambassador for his glory?

⇨ The group might need to warm up with a discussion about things that are "glorious," e.g., a sunset, a bride, a crystal clear day.

You thought your job description was to struggle through life and then die. That makes sense when you believe that your life has no bigger purpose. But if you believe you work for someone else and if you love the person you work for, you have a reason to get up in the morning. You have a reason to say no to the desires that take you away from God.

Depression experts have suggested that one reason depression is at an all-time high is that we have nothing to believe in that is bigger than ourselves. The family is breaking down; there are no noble quests. The only thing left to trust in is yourself, and, frankly, you weren't intended to carry that kind of freight.

It's no wonder you can feel so miserable when your desires are your master. You were intended to be a royal ambassador of the King.

⇨ The job description is an exalted one, but the actual outworking of it can look ordinary. We are living for God's glory when we run from addictions instead of embracing them, when we speak the truth, when we pray, when we love. Every step you take toward the Kingdom of Heaven is evidence that you are an honored ambassador.

GOD IS HOLY

Along with being your Creator, God also tells you that he is holy. Enter into the throne room of the King, and you will hear voices crying out, "Holy, holy, holy" (Isaiah 6:3; Revelation 4:8). You, too, will be saying those same words when you see the Lord face to face. They mean that God is not like his creatures. Nothing in creation can compare to him (Isaiah 40:25).

One way you have gotten into trouble in the past is by believing that God is like a regular human being, maybe only a little smarter, faster, stronger, and angrier.

People lose patience, so God must too.

People can forgive to a certain point and then enough is enough, so God must also have limits on his forgiveness toward you.

People can't see everybody at once, so God must not be able to see us when we do things in secret.

When you think such things, you are saying that God is not holy. But the truth is that God can't be compared to any human being.

When you live as though God is like his creatures, you make God smaller. Understandable, to be sure. When people encounter the true God, they fall down on their knees and are afraid for their lives. His holy majesty is overwhelming. It's perfectly natural to want to domesticate him, but who worships a tame god? Who would want to?

Life is always linked to God. You always live in a way that reveals your ultimate loyalties. Here's how God's holiness enters into the mix. When you do your addiction, you usually do it in secret. If someone important is with you, especially if it is someone who disapproves of what you do, you don't do it. This means you must believe that God is not present everywhere at all times. You must think he is someone who sees some things but not others. You aren't consciously saying this, but there are a lot of things you do without knowing the details, especially if you are living in the dark. Your real motives only come out when you get caught. When the lights go on, you discover that you didn't believe God was holy. You didn't believe he was the God who sees everything.

> O LORD, you have searched me
>   and you know me.
> You know when I sit and when I rise;
>   you perceive my thoughts from afar.
> You discern my going out and my lying down;
>   you are familiar with all my ways.
> Before a word is on my tongue
>   you know it completely, O LORD.
> You hem me in—behind and before;
>   you have laid your hand upon me.
> Such knowledge is too wonderful for me,
>   too lofty for me to attain.
> Where can I go from your Spirit?
>   Where can I flee from your presence?
> If I go up to the heavens, you are there;
>   if I make my bed in the depths, you are there.
> If I rise on the wings of the dawn,
>   if I settle on the far side of the sea,
> even there your hand will guide me,
>   your right hand will hold me fast.
> If I say, "Surely the darkness will hide me
>   and the light become night around me,"
> even the darkness will not be dark to you;
>   the night will shine like the day,
>   for darkness is as light to you. (Psalm 139:1–12)

Don't think that your heavenly parent is spying on you. People who walked with God have known that when God sees you, there is no greater blessing. Consider the famous Hebrew prayer: "The LORD make his face to shine upon you and be gracious to you; the LORD turn his face toward you and give you peace" (Numbers 6:25–26).

? You thought God didn't see, but he does, and you are blessed because of it. Any ideas on how this is a blessing to you?

What are other ways you live as if God was like an ordinary human being?

> It is time to talk about God. Set people loose. Make sure they talk more than you do.

TAKE ACTION

All true change comes from the knowledge of the true, Creator, Holy God. When you know your King and, as a result, know yourself, you are ready for battle.

Are you alert yet?

Here are some ways you can take action.

> There are a lot of options here. Not everyone will do them all, at least not right now. But point out that there are many great action steps available. That isn't intended to overwhelm anyone. After all, we are creatures who can only do one thing at a time. The point is to give hope.

Tell God how great he is. Not all your prayers will be requests and confessions. When you read the Psalms, you will notice that many of them don't have any requests at all (e.g., Psalm 29). They simply recount the greatness of God. So let the psalmists be your mentor. Tell God how great he is. Tell him what he has done in history and in your life.

What does this have to do with addictions? An affection for God expels idols. Attending worship services at your church is another way you can tell God how great he is. You might not have thought that singing worship songs was a way to do battle with addictions, but it is.

Reject secret ways. You thought God couldn't see. Read all of Psalm 139 as a way to remember that God—The Holy One—does see. This is an opportunity to clean out your actual idols or secret reminders of them: drugs, phone numbers, private Internet accounts, hidden stash.

? What would you throw away or change if you knew that someone you highly respected knew where you went and what you did?

What *will* you throw away?

How will you keep running from your old idols?

? Your secret ways include your imagination. What do you savor in your imagination that has to be thrown away? Even your innermost thoughts are apparent to God. Though your thoughts don't hurt other people quite as much, they can still reveal that you want to manage your world apart from God, and that is a big problem.

How are you doing with your thoughts and imaginations?

Confess to God. "Selfishness—self-centeredness! That, we think, is the root of our troubles," wrote Bill Wilson of AA. We can be angry with God because we feel wronged. We can ignore God because we feel neglected. We can be ferociously loyal to our own ways and interpretations because we believe that God is like an ordinary person we can choose to ignore. Whatever opinion we hold, selfishness—self-centeredness—fuels it.

Although you might have already confessed your selfishness to God, you will find that you often confess the same thing again and again. You will do that for two reasons. First, you will continue to be selfish after your first confession, so you will need to confess again. Second, you will discover new depths to your selfishness, so it will be as if you saw it for the first time.

What from this step has pricked your conscience? Speak about that to the Lord.

Confess to others. The same pattern applies to your relationships with other people. You might confess the same thing more than once because you see more of your selfishness and more of how you hurt others. When you are in an addictive trance, all you see is your addiction. When you come out of it, you begin to see God more clearly; you see other people more clearly too.

⇨ This action step appears for the first time here.

If you see more of the depths of your addiction, or more of the hurt your selfishness has caused others, ask their forgiveness.

Does anyone come to mind?

Retell your story. Try telling your story in a way that acknowledges your addiction as an idol. You worshiped it, placing it in the middle of your heart. Your actions were motivated by your own selfishness; what you really wanted was for your idol to serve your own desires. Consider what God says about idols in Isaiah 44:6–23. The story has two sides: your idols are part of the system of lies that you erected, but they are also part of the system of lies by which you were deceived.

When you retell the story, end with hope. Here is how that passage about idols ends.

> [The Lord says], "Remember these things [about the lies of idolatry], O Jacob,
>> for you are my servant, O Israel. I have made you, you are my servant;
>> O Israel, I will not forget you. I have swept away your offenses like a cloud,
> your sins like the morning mist.
> Return to me,
>> for I have redeemed you." Sing for joy, O heavens, for the LORD has done this;
>> shout aloud, O earth beneath.
> Burst into song, you mountains,
>> you forests and all your trees, for the LORD has redeemed Jacob,
> he displays his glory in Israel. (Isaiah 44:21–23)

Run to God. When you run away from addictions, run to God. Otherwise you will just be running in a big circle. One way to run to God is to come to him as the Father, knowing that there are some things you can confidently ask him. You can ask to know him better, and you can be confident that he will grant your request because that is exactly what you need and what God wants for you. Ephesians 1:17–19 (with a few pronouns changed to make it more personal) serves as a great template for such a prayer:

> Father, the God of our Lord Jesus Christ, please give me your Spirit of wisdom and revelation, so that I may know you better. I pray also that the eyes of my heart may be enlightened in order that I may know the hope to which I have been called and your incomparably great power.

Here is another prayer taken from Ephesians 3:15–19. It focuses on growth in the knowledge of God's love. Again, the pronouns are changed so that, instead of Paul praying it for his friends in Ephesus, it will be you praying it for yourself:

> Father, I pray that out of your glorious riches you may strengthen me with power through your Spirit in my inner being, so that Christ may dwell in my heart through faith. And I pray that I may have power to grasp how wide and long and high and deep is the love of Christ, and to know this love that surpasses knowledge—that I may be filled to the measure of all the fullness of God.

> Make these your prayers.

 If you want to really enjoy your time together, be like a priest and speak a blessing to the group. (Or pass the honor around to others.) The priestly blessing in Numbers 6:24–26 can get you started.

STEP 6:

Follow Jesus

MAIN IDEA: All eyes on Jesus. God has centered his plan for you and the entire universe squarely on Jesus. Follow Jesus Christ, and you will be on the real path to change.

> "What do you want?" You could begin with this question because one important goal is for you and your friends to change what you want (yes, you are more like the addict than you know).
>
> "What do you **really** want?"
>
> "What do you **want** to want?"
>
> The psalmist is way out in front of most of us, but he is a wise man we can follow and imitate. Here is his desire.
>
> One thing I ask of the LORD . . . that I may dwell in the house of the LORD all the days of my life, to gaze upon the beauty of the LORD and to seek him in his temple. (Psalm 27:4)
>
> Want this—really want it—and addictions will be a distant memory.
>
> Not all group members want this yet, but they could pray that they would become more and more like this psalmist.

Have you ever thought that Jesus is good, the Father is ticked off, and the Spirit is a thing—an impersonal force? If so, you are delving into the mysteries of how God is both three and one. The Father is God; the Son is God; the Spirit is God. But the Father is not the Son; the Son is not the Spirit; the Spirit is not the Father.* The apostle Paul says, "I keep asking that the God of our *Lord Jesus Christ*, the glorious *Father*, may give you the *Spirit* of wisdom and revelation, so that you may know him better" (Ephesians 1:17, emphasis added). Yes, it's a mystery, but that shouldn't keep us from studying and learning more. We can't get our mind around something as basic as the atom either, but scientists and students are still hard at work trying.

Here is the truth: The Father is *not* mean, the Son is much more than the nice and accepting gentle Jesus, and the Spirit is very personal. The Father is the One who runs after wayward children (Luke 15:11–32). The Son is the fullest expression of the Father's character. And the Spirit is the Spirit of Jesus: he gives us the power to change, he knows the thoughts of the Father, and he impresses the words of God onto our hearts (1 Corinthians 2:10–13). The Spirit also knows *your* thoughts and sorrows and communicates them to the Father.

---

* From John Frame, *Salvation Belongs to the Lord: An Introduction to Systematic Theology* (Phillipsburg, PA: P & R, 2006), 33.

For now, however, all eyes on Jesus. If you want to know God in the fullest way possible, look at Jesus.

After his resurrection Jesus appeared to some travelers who didn't realize who he was. They talked about Jesus, how they had hoped that he was the Messiah sent from God. They were saddened by the crucifixion and perplexed by the reports that his grave was empty. As they walked together, Jesus spoke to them.

> "How foolish you are, and how slow of heart to believe all that the prophets have spoken! Did not the Christ have to suffer these things and then enter his glory?" And beginning with Moses and all the Prophets, he explained to them what was said in all the Scriptures concerning himself. (Luke 24:25–27)

In other words, all Scripture points to Jesus. Those disciples on the road had begun to wonder where they ought to put their trust now that Jesus was gone; and Jesus said, in effect, "You fools! It's always been about Jesus. It's still about Jesus." Whatever you read in Scripture, whatever you hear in a sermon, every worship song—they all point to Jesus. And for deep change to take place, your life must point in the same direction.

You already have some idea of who Jesus is and what he did. But in any good relationship, you shouldn't be satisfied with "some idea" of who the other person is. When you get to know someone, you have some impressions that are accurate and some that aren't. You have found out some things for yourself, but you have heard conflicting reports from others. With Jesus, you have probably ended up with a blend of the true and the false. Don't you want to know him better? There is always more to learn.

JESUS THE RE-CREATOR IS REMAKING YOU (AND ALL OF CREATION)

You know that Jesus was the King born in a manger. He also created the wood for the manger. Jesus is the Creator of the universe. He is God, after all. So when he came as a man, he was up to something big. He didn't come simply to show us how to live the way we were intended to live. He came to begin nothing short of a complete *re*-creation of his universe. That re-creation includes you!

Re-creation was essential. The entire creation was in bondage; it needed liberation and renewal. The kingdom of God had been all but erased from the map. God's children felt right at home in the midst of darkness and lies. They didn't feel the need for a way out. They—we—needed completely new hearts.

Everyone needs to be re-created. All we have to do is look at ourselves to know that something dramatic needed to happen.

God spoke of this coming re-creation throughout the Old Testament, hundreds of years before Jesus came to earth. In the Book of Jeremiah, for instance, God describes a new start for his people. Just a few clarifications before we look at this beautiful, hope-filled passage. In these verses God speaks in terms of a covenant, which is a legally binding agreement or oath. It consists of promises made by both parties. The covenant God originally brokered had been shredded by humanity's rebellion against him. In this passage God says that he will make a new covenant through Jesus Christ. (Actually, this is his way of keeping his *original* promise, even though we didn't.) The fact that it is with "the house of Israel and the house of Judah" doesn't mean that it is exclusively for them. Instead, it means that the agreement that brought the promised Messiah is made *through* them. They, in turn, give the Messiah to the world.

> "The time is coming," declares the LORD,
>   "when I will make a new covenant
> with the house of Israel
>   and with the house of Judah.
> It will not be like the covenant
>   I made with their forefathers
> when I took them by the hand
>   to lead them out of Egypt,
> because they broke my covenant,
>   though I was a husband to them,"
>   declares the LORD.
> "This is the covenant I will make with the house of Israel
>   after that time," declares the LORD.

"I will put my law in their minds
    and write it on their hearts.
I will be their God,
    and they will be my people.
No longer will a man teach his neighbor,
    or a man his brother, saying, 'Know the LORD,'
because they will all know me,
    from the least of them to the greatest,"
    declares the LORD.
"For I will forgive their wickedness
    and will remember their sins no more."
                  (Jeremiah 31:31–34)

A new heart. Forgiveness that goes all the way to your deep-seated shame and guilt. If you want to leave your addiction, those are the things you need. God has invited you to receive them. But remember, even though this is a *new* covenant, it is still a covenant, so God does require a couple of things of you.

First, you must recognize that you really do *need* both forgiveness and a new heart. Otherwise, you would have no reason to come to him. You would be coming to browse but not to stay.

Do you believe that?

Second, you must recognize that you have nothing to bring to this agreement. You don't have perfect contrition, perfect motives, a radically changed life, or anything else you can give to God. *The requirement is that you bring nothing.* That way it's clear to everyone, including you, that Jesus has done it all, and Jesus alone is worshiped. When you bring nothing, you bring glory to God.

When you have messed up, it is easy to believe that you have to balance that out with something good. Then, you think, it is okay to come to Jesus. That, however, is not reality. You can only come to Jesus when you know you have nothing good to bring to him. That should be easy, but you will find that it is more difficult than you think.

"The time is coming," said the prophet, when heaven is going to penetrate earth. That time came when Jesus entered the world. The rest of your life will be an opportunity to understand more about what happened when he did.

? This passage from Jeremiah told what was going to happen when Jesus came. How would you put into words what happened when Jesus came? What difference does that make for your addiction?

> The more your friends talk about God the better. Listen to them and be blessed by what they have to say.

Here is another word to you from the Lord, saying much the same thing.

> "'This is what the Sovereign LORD says: I will gather you from the nations and bring you back from the countries where you have been scattered. . . .' They will return to it [their homeland] and remove all its vile images and detestable idols. I will give them an undivided heart and put a new spirit in them; I will remove from them their heart of stone and give them a heart of flesh. Then they will follow my decrees and be careful to keep my laws. They will be my people, and I will be their God." (Ezekiel 11:17–20)

It's not hard to find yourself in this. You were scattered; you had a divided heart, cherished your idols, and were not careful to follow the commands of the King. Through the re-creation that Jesus brought about, you have the power to change. But it doesn't come through sheer willpower. A heart transplant is the only answer, and you receive a new heart when you surrender and say that *Jesus* is Lord instead of you.

Then, after you have received your new heart, you maintain and revive it as you say daily that Jesus is Lord instead of you.

? Is there any reason why you would resist such an offer?

JESUS CHRIST PAID YOUR WAY OUT OF BONDAGE**

Here are the details of what Jesus did. You know he died on a cross, and you have heard he rose from the dead. Now you should know what his death and resurrection mean for you and your present struggle.

** When you speak of Jesus Christ, Jesus is his given name and Christ is his role. (Christ is the Greek name for "Messiah.") It is the same as saying Jesus the King.

It might seem a little late in the process to start talking about Jesus, but you had to make the connection between addiction and God before the cross of Jesus Christ would make real sense.

You deserved death. The cross and its brutality don't make sense if you don't understand that your rebellion against God deserves death. He is the Holy King. Even human societies know that insurrection against a king deserves punishment. How much more when that rebellion is against God! When you try to manage your world apart from God, you have committed treason, and the penalty for treason is death. (*Sin* is the word that is commonly used to identify our treasonous acts).

The word **sin** finally makes its first appearance. All along you have been talking about sin, but not necessarily using the word. Does the word jolt anyone? It might have if it had appeared on the first page, but it shouldn't now.

This is the critical point. You need to get this. Minimize sin and you minimize God. Minimize God and you are easing your way back into your addictive world. Too often the process of change breaks down right here.

Why does God care about a few extra beers, a brief food binge, or five minutes on a porn site? Because they are all expressions of false worship and misplaced loyalties. With them, you are saying, "I want to *be* god—at least for the next few minutes—rather than trust and obey God." You are exiting the back door of the Kingdom of Heaven and returning to your old haunts in the darkness.

In your sin, you elevate yourself above God.

You say that he is a liar when you say that your sin is not as bad as he says it is.

You accuse him of stinginess; you think you can find something better in a different kingdom, in spite of the fact that he offers you the whole kingdom—not just a little piece, but the whole thing!

You also feel miserable, of course. But don't confuse feeling miserable with an acknowledgment of your sin. Although they might be related, bad feelings can come when other people are disappointed with you. That is not the same as acknowledging that your sin is ultimately against God.

Can you distinguish between the two?

When you wander into the dark kingdom, it is hard to see your own motives clearly. But what you really are doing when you follow your own desires is making yourself an enemy of God. You have tossed him aside.

It sounds harsh, but it should also sound true. If you are fuzzy about this, get help. Does it feel like too much condemnation? It should be sobering, no doubt. But this is reality. This is the way things truly are. If your friend had a disease that would be lethal if left untreated, he would be thankful when you diagnosed it accurately. He might not be happy with the diagnosis, but he would know that the diagnosis is the first step toward healing.

Sin is your most serious diagnosis. The treatment is that Jesus voluntarily took on himself the penalty for your sin. Your sin has been paid for. You don't have to be paralyzed by fear any longer (and there is a lot of fear that feeds your addiction). So don't hold back from seeing the ugliness, arrogance, and treachery of your sin. Be willing to see it clearly. It will only make the treatment that much more beautiful.

? Do you believe that your sin deserves punishment and the wrath of God? Put your own words on that reality.

> Challenge your friends to speak about the seriousness of sin, but with hope—always with hope.

Jesus Christ paid the penalty of sin and turned away God's anger. When you really look at the cross and the entire Hebrew sacrificial system that pointed to Jesus' sacrifice, you can tell that someone was angry. The sacrificial system throughout the Old Testament was all about bloody carcasses. Blood was everywhere. This was God's anger being poured out, but not on those who deserved it. When history finally gets to the cross, you find that Jesus was "crushed" for your sins (Isaiah 53:5). "Now he has appeared once for all at the end of the ages to do away with sin by the sacrifice of himself" (Hebrews 9:26). He was even forsaken by his Father so that you wouldn't have to be

(Psalm 22:1). God decided to allow a substitute to take our place. The surprise is that the substitute was the King himself.

It all seems much too good to be true, which actually hints that it *must* be true. It's the sort of thing nobody would have made up. Think about it: if you were going to make up a myth about God, would it really involve God becoming a man and sacrificing himself? Wouldn't a made-up God just be a bigger version of an ordinary person—sort of a superman—but still, a version of us? No one could have invented what God actually did. If some ancient wise man was going to invent a religious system, he certainly wouldn't have dreamed this up. God becomes man and takes the penalty for sin on himself because he is both just in his judgments and extravagant in his love. You will find nothing like this anywhere else.

What you *do* find in other religions are systems in which you repay the god or gods when you are bad. Disappoint the gods, you get whacked. You have to figure out some way to pay the gods back for whatever you did to offend them.

Sound familiar? There's a good chance that you have some of those systems operating in your own head. That's why you don't turn quickly to God when you mess up. You think he is going to whack you. You think you have to pay him back for what you have done.

We all have a mixture of truth and error in our beliefs. God's truth is spliced together with what you think *should* be true.

What do you think *should* be true? Most people believe two laws: you get what you deserve, and you don't get something for nothing. When you blend the truth about God's forgiveness and mercy with the lies of these two laws, you get a guilt-producing mixture that actually opposes what God really did and said.

Does this make sense? It is important because anything that detracts from God's goodness becomes an excuse to turn away from him, and you can't afford to do that.

It's a reasonable assumption: you believe you have to pay God back for what you have done. That makes sense if you are thinking like an ordinary human. You have to "pay to play." But it is absurd when you really know both God and yourself.

First of all, you are overestimating your ability to repay God. Spiritually, you are broke, and the penalty you owe is death. Second, you are underestimating the love and complete forgiveness God showed you at the cross of Christ. All he asks you to do—and all you *can* do—is nothing. Just say thank you and acknowledge that God alone deserves your trust, allegiance, and obedience. Any other path might have a few temporary thrills along the way, but it is a path careening toward death.

? How have you tried to pay God back? Some try feeling especially sorry, even depressed. Others promise to never do it again. What have you come up with?

Jesus Christ set you free from captivity to sin, Satan, and your idols. Much more happened at the cross than you realize. Forgiveness is great, but it's not enough if you are left in bondage to the trifecta of your idols, your lusts, and Satan himself, the personal power behind all things anti-God.

> Don't you know that when you offer yourselves to someone to obey him as slaves, you are slaves to the one whom you obey—whether you are slaves to sin, which leads to death, or to obedience, which leads to righteousness? (Romans 6:16)

Through Jesus' death on the cross, the Father "has rescued us from the dominion of darkness and brought us into the kingdom of the Son he loves, in whom we have redemption, the forgiveness of sins" (Colossians 1:13–14). Death breaks all claims that were made on you or your estate. When Jesus died on the cross, he broke the chokehold that the dark kingdom had over us.

Of course, God doesn't free you from prison and leave you on your own to fend for yourself. He brings you back to where you were intended to be in the first place. You were intended to be a child of God, not a child of darkness, and he bought you back to give you that kind of life.

There it is. The world is structured according to kingdoms. You are either in the kingdom of darkness or the kingdom of God. Your addiction showed that you preferred to spend time in the kingdom of darkness. But now, when you say that Jesus is Lord and King, you are identifying the *rightful* center of your life and your allegiance to God's kingdom. When you say that and believe that the King is now alive, you show that you have received a new heart.

? Are you ready to do that? Wisdom is about action. If you believe this to be true, you should respond. What are you ready to do or say? What does it actually mean to take the path away from darkness and to the Kingdom of Jesus Christ?

⇨ "Wake up," "respond," "do something"— wisdom comes by trust in a person more than the accumulation of information, and trust in the person of Christ leads to action.

Maybe you have already said that Jesus is Lord. If so, you can say it again. Whether this is the first time you turned to Jesus or the hundredth, everyone does the same thing. The first time you turn, it is called conversion. The hundredth time, it is called repentance.

So you see that your problem goes deeper than your actual addictive behavior. The problem is that you think your life is your own! Of course, your life *can* be your own if all you want is death. But when your eyes have seen the King, how could you want death and misery? When you are invited to the banquet that will satisfy you to the depths of your soul, how could you settle for poverty and starvation?

? "You are not your own; you were bought at a price" (1 Corinthians 6:19–20). "He died for all, that those who live should no longer live for themselves but for him who died for them and was raised again" (2 Corinthians 5:15). How would your life be different if you acted that way? Wouldn't it be nice if someone you trusted could have control for a change?

Do you give up? Surrender? Lay down your arms and bow down to the true King? Do you want Jesus Christ? If so, then you are not your own anymore. No more unilateral decisions. Every time you go back to your addictions, you are saying that you want to belong to yourself. You don't want to go there anymore. Do you?

The cross seems like a peculiar entry point into real life. But it is the gate that opens the path to the Kingdom.

- The cross shows that God is just in the way he deals with sin. Sin deserves punishment, and at the cross it receives punishment.
- The cross displays sacrificial love beyond anything we have ever experienced from other human beings. This certainly calls our attention to the glory of God.
- The cross shows how God triumphed over Satan and his kingdom. Cruel kings use their power to kill, but Jesus Christ took that power out of Satan's hands when he died in our place.

JESUS *THE* MAN SHOWS YOU HOW TO BE HUMAN

The last thing you should know about Jesus is that he was both The God and The Man. Study Jesus and you will learn what human beings were intended to look like. He will show you the way to true humanness. He told the truth. He loved others. He felt joy deeply. He felt sorrow deeply, too, because he entered fully into life.

When you are imitating someone other than Jesus, it's like running a gas-powered car on vegetable oil. It just doesn't work. When we live contrary to the way we were created, the result is misery, with only brief glimpses of what it would be like to be fully human.

This is why it is so important for you to read the Gospel stories about Jesus. He is the King on a mission. He is remaking his people so that they actually look more and more like him. He is always telling people to follow him, to imitate him. When you were in darkness, you had no power to follow him. When you turn in his direction, it is evidence that his power is working in you, so let the re-creation process begin.

? Imagine on paper what a *truly* human life would look like.

TAKE ACTION

Are you awake? Remember, there is no neutral ground in this battle.

Hope check: Where are you on a scale of 1 to 10?

1	2	3	4	5	6	7	8	9	10

Hopelessness   Hope

Here are some ways you can take action.

Come. Say yes. Run to Jesus. God says, "This is my Son, whom I love; with him I am well pleased. Listen to him!" (Matthew 17:5). Jesus is God and Christ, so his words have authority. Listen to him. Jesus said,

> "Come to me, all you who are weary and burdened, and I will give you rest. Take my yoke upon you and learn from me, for I am gentle and humble in heart, and you will find rest for your souls." (Matthew 11:28–29)

When you receive an invitation, you should respond. Not to respond is to refuse the invitation; it is the same as a no. With this invitation, you don't have to do anything but say, "Yes. Thank you for your invitation. I humbly accept."

Will you come? Given such an invitation, it is hard to imagine why you wouldn't. The only requirement mentioned in this passage is that you should feel weary and burdened.

? How are you feeling weary and burdened?

? When you run to him, you are running away from addiction. What does it mean to come to him? Better yet, what does it mean to *run* to him?

Say no. Run from anything connected with death. When two invitations come for the same date, saying yes to one means saying no to the other. Your other invitation, of course, comes from your own desires, which have the stench of the grave on them.

? What will you say no to?

Which people?
What places?
What activities?
What imaginations?

"No" seems easy, but you know that is not the case. In fact, if you don't practice saying no long before temptations are upon you, your temptations could easily overwhelm you, and you will revert to your robotic state.

? What do you need to say no to today?

? In the darkness you are isolated; on God's path you are part of a community. Who can you tell about these things?

Let the cross have the final word. All true change must go through the cross because nothing but the sacrifice and the resurrection of Jesus has enough power to bring about real change. Otherwise, you will be stuck in guilt. And guilt won't change you.

> The cross says that the kingdom of darkness no longer has power over you (Galatians 1:4).
> The cross paid your way out of Satan's domain (Mark 10:45).
> The cross is where God has rescued his people in a way that demonstrated his sacrificial love so convincingly that it can never be fairly questioned again (John 3:16).
> The cross says that the penalty for the sin you just confessed has been *paid*. It doesn't have to be paid *ever* again (Hebrews 9:11–13).
> The cross says that your sins are forgiven (Ephesians 1:7).
> The cross is the place where your sin and sickness are healed (Matthew 8:16–17).
> The cross says that Jesus has done it all, so there is no place for pride (Galatians 6:14).
> The cross is the reason you have life, and you now live for the One who died for you (2 Corinthians 5:15).
> The cross guarantees hope and joy for those who put their trust in Jesus instead of themselves.

? Now put your own words on what the cross of Jesus really means.

Here is how you get to the cross: When you are facing your addiction, *turn around*.

> This action step appears as one among many, but it is the one that is most important.
>
> "For I resolved to know nothing while I was with you except Jesus Christ and him crucified." (1 Corinthians 2:2)
>
> Earlier you read that all change is personal and must go through God and the true knowledge of him. This is more specific. God has revealed himself most fully in Jesus Christ, and the mission of Jesus can be summarized by the cross. The new retellings of your friends' stories can have the cross at the center.

Pray. When you say yes to God's invitation, you have prayed. Here is more you can say.

Lord, you are patient and kind. You don't treat me as my sins deserve. How do you do it? How can you love and forgive me? It certainly isn't because I deserve love and forgiveness from you. It can only be because that is who you are. Lord, forgive me, and teach me more about yourself, so I can be the person you intended me to be. I am humbled by your greatness and your love.

STEP 7:

Have a Plan

MAIN IDEA: Every battle needs a plan. A plan shows that you have hope and are eager for change. It won't be foolproof, but it is essential.

> Plans don't make us acceptable to God. They don't liberate us. You make plans **after** you are liberated, not before. Your plans are your response to what God has already done. As important as plans are, you don't trust in a plan. You trust in a person. Group members can remind each other of that as they develop more specific plans.
>
> For further reading, consider chapter 11 of **Addictions—A Banquet in the Grave**.

An army is facing the critical battle of the war.

"General, what is your plan?"

"Well, son, I thought we would have a late breakfast and then engage the enemy."

"But what is your plan?"

"That is my plan."

That, of course, is a plan for defeat.

The battle is on. At every step, a path veers off into danger and death, and you are no expert at map reading—at least not yet. You are better able to discern the difference between the two paths, but the bad one can still sound good. That's the battle.

When you simply give in to your cravings, there is no battle. Your loyalties are clear. But now you are saying that your addiction is the enemy. Your selfish desires, your idols, and Satan—all are enemies.

The problem is that old masters don't let go easily. When you come to Jesus Christ, you don't suddenly enter a demilitarized zone between yourself and the object of your temptations. Instead, your temptations are in hot pursuit of you, and they fight dirty. They pretend they are life itself, but they are death.

"Let go and let God" is not going to cut it. As a *true* human who has the Spirit of God, you go off into battle against sin. What you know about these battles is that you will gain ground in small increments: one foot of enemy turf taken back, then another; one step on the right path, then another. Small setbacks are common, too, but you have been promised victory and you have the momentum on your side.

Every small setback is an opportunity to go back into the war room—a.k.a. the cross—and, with the help of others, shore up your strategy for battle.

Here is an encouraging word from Martin Luther, one of the better known of your fellow battlers.

> Christian living does not mean to *be* good but to become good; not to *be* well but to get well; not being but becoming; not rest but training. We are not yet, but we shall be. It has not yet happened. But it is the way. Not everything shines and sparkles as yet, but everything is getting better.*

You have a plan. Otherwise you wouldn't be considering these steps. What is your plan?

"I'm going to head straight for the cross."

Sounds good, but you still need specifics.

SET UP BOUNDARIES

If your idol is crack, you know where you can buy it. Does your dealer still have your phone number? Have you changed it? Do you ever go alone to places where crack might be available? Your goal is to establish boundaries—unscalable barriers between yourself and the object of your affection. .

> Like a city whose walls are broken down
>   is a man who lacks self-control. (Proverbs 25:28)

If computer pornography is your idol, have you signed up with a service to inform a friend of every site you hit? Of course, ways around barriers exist no matter how high you erect them, but they are still necessary. They might slow you down just long enough to hear the voice of wisdom. What other computers do you use? Have you told the owners of those computers that you can't use them anymore because you too easily give in to your temptations? Is your own computer in a public place?

---

* Cited in Douglas John Hall, *The Cross in Our Context* (Minneapolis: Fortress, 2003), 109.

"If your right eye causes you to sin, gouge it out and throw it away. It is better for you to lose one part of your body than for your whole body to be thrown into hell. And if your right hand causes you to sin, cut it off and throw it away. It is better for you to lose one part of your body than for your whole body to go into hell." (Matthew 5:29–30)

When you sit to dine with a ruler,
    note well what is before you,
and put a knife to your throat
    if you are given to gluttony. (Proverbs 23:1–2)

The apostle Paul modified the warfare imagery and used an athletic one. (Athletics were the way to prepare for warfare.)

Do you not know that in a race all the runners run, but only one gets the prize? Run in such a way as to get the prize. Everyone who competes in the games goes into strict training. They do it to get a crown that will not last; but we do it to get a crown that will last forever. Therefore I do not run like a man running aimlessly; I do not fight like a man beating the air. No, I beat my body and make it my slave so that after I have preached to others, I myself will not be disqualified for the prize. (1 Corinthians 9:24–27)

Now *those* are plans. Scripture is exaggerating to make a point, but the point is well taken. You must be ruthless.

Up to this point you have been asked to run from anything associated with secrets, lies, darkness, and death. You have been assembling the pieces of a plan. Now you need to put those pieces together into a larger strategy. If you don't have such a plan, get help. This is new to you. It is unfamiliar. Don't expect to be an expert strategist immediately. Consult with those who have more experience than you do.

How long will the plan need to be in force? Some elements of the plan will be there for life. But there is something you should know about lust and craving. As long as you aren't feeding them at the level of your imagination, and as long as you are committed to battling them, the cravings tend to die down over time. They might not be silent, but they won't be screaming at you all day long.

? You erected some boundaries in the last few steps. What are they? Are they as strong as they can possibly be?

> We can sabotage any plan. That's easy. The plan that works best is one that your friends devise for themselves. Caution them about making a plan for **you** rather than them. You and others, of course, will offer counsel about the plan, but keep your friends active. They want to develop a plan that is within their reach and in harmony with what the Spirit is teaching them.

INCLUDE PEOPLE

Your strategy must include avoiding privacy. You are going to be as public as possible about your fight. You are going to include people in everything—as many people as possible. They will review your plan, they will hear your honest confession and spiritual doubts, they will pass on wisdom, they will remind you of what Jesus did, and they will pray for you.

Your home base for relationships will be a local church. Granted, people in the church sometimes look worse than people outside the church, but that should make you feel at home. You will have to be patient and forbearing with them, and they will have to be patient and forbearing with you. Yes, expect sin to come to the surface. When it does, remember that God uses messed-up people for his service. It makes him look even better. If God only used perfect people (of which there are none), it would undermine his plan to do powerful work through very ordinary ones.

In recent times, addicts have found sanctuary in AA more than in a local church. Sometimes those in AA can be more understanding than those in the church. When it comes to really knowing what you feel, AA members are *definitely* more understanding. But don't forget what is really happening at church.

- This is your family, and it is closer than genetic ties. You have been joined with them by the blood of Christ. Someday you will have a perfect love for them and they for you.
- This is where people are gathered in the name of Jesus, and the Spirit promises to be present at such gatherings.

- This is where you worship, which is the most potent weapon of all for fighting addictions.
- This is where you will be reminded of Christ who was crucified for you.
- This is where you can serve other people in the name of Jesus.
- This is where you can know people and pray for them. They need you.
- This is where you will have brothers and sisters who pray for you and with you. You need them.
- This is where you will find fellow idolaters who are all in the process of learning to flee and even hate their idolatry.

You can err in at least two ways when you meet with the body of Christ. One is that you will feel different from everyone else. You will look around and see people who seem to have their acts together, and you will feel completely out of place. But these are lies. You aren't seeing accurately. When you look around in church, you are seeing a bunch of people who have been wounded in battle. The church is a hospital for spiritually sick and wounded people. It is just the place for you.

The other way you can err is to stand in judgment of people in the church. You might criticize their ignorance about addictions, the impractical nature of the teaching and preaching, the hypocrisy. You might tell yourself that you are being honest while everyone else is just pretending to have it together.

Both errors are lures from the dark kingdom. Satan's bait is to take small kernels of truth and use them for his purposes. If you move away from God's people, you are most likely moving away from God.

? How are you doing with a local church?

How can you improve this part of your strategy?

 It can be easy to stay within the cozy confines of an accepting group. But it might be time for your friends to branch out. Are there other people who can be told the new and improved story? We move toward other people because we all need help, but your friends will also bless other people—just as they have blessed you.

BE ALERT TO YOUR IMAGINATIONS

As you put together your plan, don't skip your imaginations. One reason cravings can last so long is that people stop their addiction but continue to savor it in their own minds. Remember, God cares about what you do on the outside, but he cares equally about what is going on inside, in the theater of your mind.

Your plan can't just be, "I won't think about it anymore." Scripture offers more penetrating and effective strategies. Certainly, you will have stray thoughts about your addiction—you don't encourage them; they just pop into your head. While it would be wise to mention those to someone, it might not be worth engaging those thoughts in a fight. There is a difference between a stray thought and a nurtured one. With the strays, you can send them away by focusing on the task at hand, whether that be work, rest, or caring about family and friends.

But there are other times when it might be wise to pause and ask what your imagination is really saying. Do you love your old addiction? If so, part of your strategy would be to place it under the bright lights for questioning until the truth becomes apparent.

What is the state of your imaginations?

What will be your plan with your imagination?

DEVELOP YOUR IMAGINATION

There are many "don'ts" in Scripture because we do many things that are against God. You need authoritative direction on what not to do. But alongside those don'ts are the "dos" and the "betters." *Do* love; *do* truth telling. Jesus is *better* than anyone anticipated: his promises are better than you could imagine; the cross is better—and more crammed with meaning—than you will ever know; his love is better than life itself; and his plan for your future is better than you could imagine.

Let God's Word unleash your imagination. Consider, for example, the promise that you will one day be spiritually perfect if you receive Jesus as Lord:

How great is the love the Father has lavished on us, that we
should be called children of God! And that is what we are!
. . . Dear friends, now we are children of God, and what we
will be has not yet been made known. But we know that
when he appears, we shall be like him, for we shall see him
as he is. Everyone who has this hope in him purifies himself, just as he is pure. (1 John 3:1–2)

In other words, you are destined to be without sin. Sin is an intruder.
It will cling to you until its last gasp, but it is on its way out. The day is
coming when you will be without sin.

Now imagine that—and it *will* take some imagination. Perfect love.
Perfect worship. No more divided heart. No more tugs from the wrong
things. No more falls. Perfect unity. No jealousies. No deceptions. No
more idolatry. No more guilt or shame. There won't be any need for
perfect forgiveness because no one will be sinning against you and you
won't be sinning against God.

Talk about it. Imagine it together. It can be great fun, but it is much
more than a game. As you hope or imagine, you are actually being *given*
more grace from God that will change you. "Everyone who has this
hope in him purifies himself" (1 John 3:3).

> This one is just fun. It provides a break from self-examination and
> reminds us that the story is only going to get better.

REMEMBER

Of all the directions God gives you, "remember" may be the one he
repeats most often. Part of the human condition is that you forget spiritual reality. You forget that life is about kingdom loyalties, that you
enter the kingdom by giving up rather than by doing good and that the
road to the kingdom must go through the cross. You forget that there is
reason for both fear and peace.

"Remember" is a critical battle directive. It will point the way when
you have those crossroads experiences. To accomplish it, you are given
the Spirit, who puts the words of God in your heart. You are also given
other people who remind you of reality with their stories, their rebukes,
their encouragement, and their simple presence.

See to it, brothers, that none of you has a sinful, unbelieving heart that turns away from the living God. But encourage one another daily, as long as it is called Today, so that none of you may be hardened by sin's deceitfulness. (Hebrews 3:12–13)

? How will you jog your memory with spiritual reality?

What will you remember?
How will you help other people remember?

TAKE ACTION

Are you fully awake?

Are you afraid in a good way? Afraid of yourself?

Write out your plan. What is your plan? You want it to be as fool-proof as possible. Write it out, pass it out for evaluation, post it on your refrigerator, and revise it as needed. It will include everything from, "I will never drive near Tenth and Diamond," to "I will memorize Psalm 23." Be sure to include areas where you are vulnerable. And be sure to put Jesus in the center of it.

Be prepared for doubts. It can be difficult when you wake up every day and realize you have to fight the same old battle again and again. You get tired and start to doubt God's power. You might even wonder if all this is real. When the doubts come, don't take someone else's word for it. Get into Scripture and feed on it until you have encountered God yourself. All of Scripture is God's Word to you. When you don't know where to start, read through one of the Gospels about the life of Jesus: Matthew, Mark, Luke, or John.

You might face intrusive doubts for many reasons. One of the most obvious is simply that you think your life looks no different from the way it looked when you tried less Christ-focused approaches to deal with addictions. You had cravings before; you have cravings now. *Where,* you wonder, *is the power of God?*

The steps you have taken assume that the struggle will remain. If the struggle simply vanished, *then* you would have a reason for doubt. God's way consists of you knowing him and stubbornly turning to him every time you get spun around the other way.

Nobody claimed this was going to be easy. Instead, the way is marked by fears and battle and desperate pleas for mercy. But if you open your eyes, you will be able to see the goodness of the Lord. The struggle itself is evidence. Any steps you have taken so far are evidence. These are a result of the work of the Spirit in you.

If the doubts continue, be sure to talk with others. Ask them to tell you their stories about meeting Jesus. Ask them how they are seeing the greatness of God. Ask them how Jesus surprises them.

In emergencies, confess your selfishness and sin. That usually brings more clarity. Doubts usually have the devil's fingerprints on them, and the humility that comes with confession is a key weapon against such attacks.

? When do your doubts come?

What do they say?

Can you hear any lies in them?

Remember that the battle is good. It will feel unnatural at first. If you didn't experience a battle, it would mean that you were still on the path that leads to death. You would be tempted to go it on your own, which is what got you into trouble in the first place. The battle reminds you that you need Jesus. The battle is good.

As your friends talk more and more about spiritual things, they will learn how to communicate in a new way. But their new skill at spiritual communication can also be a cover-up. You always want to work to create an environment where the truth is prized and everyone is appropriately suspicious of their own hearts. Attract and warn: those are your two strategies.

Read Scripture. The Bible is food for the hungry and desperate.

Remember how the LORD your God led you all the way in the desert these forty years, to humble you and to test you in order to know what was in your heart, whether or not you would keep his commands. He humbled you, causing you to hunger and then feeding you with manna, which neither you nor your fathers had known, to teach you that man does not live on bread alone but on every word that comes from the mouth of the LORD. (Deuteronomy 8:2–3)

This passage is loaded. God makes his people hungry, and then he feeds them. God takes his people out into the wilderness where there will be temptations, so difficult circumstances should come as no surprise. Those temptations serve a deeper purpose: they reveal whether or not we listen to the Lord and follow him. Even more, they teach us to rely on the words of God.

? Are you reading Scripture? Are you reading it on your own?

Are God's words becoming your food?
Why? Why not?

Pray. Prayer is still your most powerful weapon. John Owen, a seventeenth-century preacher who thought long and hard about temptation, said, "Let him who would spend little time in temptation spend much time in prayer."**

Lord Jesus, I am weary. I need strength to persevere. Would you give me more of your Spirit so I can think and live like you? I want my desires changed so that what I once loved I begin to hate. I want to know what it means to find rest in you.

⇨ You can bless your friends with these words: "You are not your own; you were bought at a price" (1 Corinthians 6:19–20). There are other words too. Keep your eyes open in Scripture for good words—benedictions—you want to pray for the men or women in the group. But don't be the sole person to offer a priestly blessing. If you are in a group, let different people pray a prayer of blessing for the others.

** John Owen, *Temptation Resisted and Repulsed*, abridged by Richard Rushing (Carlisle, PA: Banner of Truth, 2007), 67.

STEP 8:

Love Others

MAIN IDEA: Relationship problems can both cause addiction and result from addiction. When you develop skills in love and reconciliation, you are doing more to resist your temptations than you realize.

> A group is much more than a resource for accountability. It is a community that is practicing kingdom values. When you confess your sin and your need, when you say yes to Jesus, when you tell others the truth about Jesus Christ, you are actually living life in the kingdom.
>
> Sometimes it is difficult to see how people are walking toward the kingdom. To put it another way, it is hard to see how the kingdom is coming to people in the group. So much struggle and misery are all around. One of the tasks of the group is to realize that Jesus has risen from the dead and he is now the King. Therefore, there will be opportunities to see the power of the kingdom at work in humble men and women. Be sure to point it out when you see it.
>
> Here is a prayer about Jesus Christ. It is a prayer you speak in the presence of the King. You are proclaiming his greatness to him, to others, and to yourself.

Praise the Lord.
　　Praise the Lord, O my soul.
I will praise the Lord all my life;
　　I will sing praise to my God as long as I live. . . .
Blessed is he whose help is the God of Jacob,
　　whose hope is in the Lord his God,
the Maker of heaven and earth,
　　the sea, and everything in them—
　　the Lord, who remains faithful forever.
He upholds the cause of the oppressed
　　and gives food to the hungry.
　　The Lord sets prisoners free,
the Lord gives sight to the blind,
　　the Lord lifts up those who are bowed down,
the Lord loves the righteous.

The Lord watches over the alien
　　and sustains the fatherless and the widow,
　　but he frustrates the ways of the wicked.
The Lord reigns forever,
　　your God, O Zion, for all generations.
　　Praise the Lord.

                                        (Psalm 146:1–2, 5–10)

When AA guides you in self-evaluation, it tells you to start with your own selfishness and then consider its most common expression: resentment.

> Resentment is the "number one" offender. It destroys more alcoholics than anything else.*

Life is about relationships. How often have you gone back to an addiction because of problems in a relationship? For some, the addiction is not the primary problem; it is only a sinful way of dealing with relationship problems—it is a way of managing relationships, or the lack of relationships, apart from God.

That's why dealing with relationships needs to be part of your plan.

RELATIONSHIPS IN WHICH YOU HAVE BEEN HURT

God's Word knows real life. It assumes that you have hurt others, but it also knows that you have *been hurt* by the indifference and selfishness of other people. With this in mind, God's first word to you when you start thinking about your relationships is "Comfort." God is the Good Shepherd who seeks and comforts his sheep.

> He tends his flock like a shepherd:
> > He gathers the lambs in his arms
> > and carries them close to his heart;
> > he gently leads those that have young. (Isaiah 40:11)

> "'As a shepherd looks after his scattered flock when he is with them, so will I look after my sheep. I will rescue them from all the places where they were scattered on a day of clouds and darkness. I will bring them out from the nations and gather them from the countries, and I will bring them into their own land. . . . There they will lie down in good grazing land, and there they will feed in a rich pasture on the mountains of Israel. I myself will tend my sheep and have them lie down, declares the Sovereign LORD. I will search for the lost and bring back the strays. I will bind up

---

* *Alcoholics Anonymous* (New York: Alcoholics Anonymous World Services, Inc., 1976), 64.

the injured and strengthen the weak, but the sleek and the strong I will destroy. I will shepherd the flock with justice."
(Ezekiel 34:12–16)

Do you see what just happened in that passage? The Shepherd comforts both the sheep who followed him and the sheep who strayed. He doesn't punish the strays. He brings them back. He heals their hurts. The tenderness of this passage is amazing.

The apostle Paul knew a lot about suffering, which means he had ample opportunity to learn about comfort.

Praise be to the God and Father of our Lord Jesus Christ, the Father of compassion and the God of all comfort, who comforts us in all our troubles, so that we can comfort those in any trouble with the comfort we ourselves have received from God. For just as the sufferings of Christ flow over into our lives, so also through Christ our comfort overflows.
(2 Corinthians 1:3–5)

Maybe you are wondering where this comfort is. If you haven't found it yet, hold on to these words because they *are* God's words to you. Go ahead, ask God for his comfort. Then keep your eyes open for it because it will come.

? Have you noticed any comfort from God yet in your life? If so, what did it look like?

While you are doing that, let's take a closer look at some of those hurts. As you think back on your hurts and resentments, you will notice that some of them are intertwined with your own pride and selfishness. Sort those out first.

Hurt from your own pride. A husband tried his best to love his wife and only expected one thing in return: that she encourage him by telling him good things about him. Every husband, certainly, likes to hear his wife tell him good things, so there was nothing wrong with his desire. The problem came when his desire grew too big and began to take the shape of an idol.

Some desires start out small. The problem comes when they are fed and grow into demands—we call them "needs" to make them sound better.

With this particular man, his anger signaled that his desires had become demands. His anger said, "I *demand* that you encourage me. If you don't, I am going to punish you with my anger." The line between "want" and "demand" is thin. When in doubt, assume that your anger is a disguised selfish demand.

> What causes fights and quarrels among you? Don't they come from your desires that battle within you? You want something but don't get it. . . . You adulterous people, don't you know that friendship with the world is hatred toward God? Anyone who chooses to be a friend of the world becomes an enemy of God. . . . Submit yourselves, then, to God. Resist the devil, and he will flee from you. Come near to God and he will come near to you. . . . Grieve, mourn and wail. Change your laughter to mourning and your joy to gloom. Humble yourselves before the Lord, and he will lift you up. (James 4:1–2, 4, 7–10)

See the connection to God again? You are ticked off at somebody. You thought it was between only you and that other person, but it isn't. Anger is almost always a sign that you demand something and you aren't getting what you demand.

? Why does this passage say that quarrelsome people are adulterous?

⇨ Life is about allegiances. This time the image, by way of the reference to adultery, is the more intimate picture of marriage rather than the cosmic story of kingdoms.

What does it mean that you are a friend of the world and an enemy of God? This is strong language!

⇨ The world (a.k.a. the kingdom of the earth, or kingdom of darkness), our own self-serving desires, and Satan—they have banded together against the Lord. The "world" is the anti-God messages that come to us in everyday life. In this case, the world says, "You deserve what you want! You have your rights!"

Notice how change begins when you submit yourself to God. Do you see the connection between quarrels and your relationship with God, even if you were not thinking about God at all?

▷ The nature of sin is that it blinds us to what is happening in our relationship with God.

If you need more clarity, look at Jesus. Although he certainly got angry when he saw oppression, he was never angry when it was about himself.

▷ In this, Jesus wasn't simply being nice. He was showing us wisdom. He was showing us how life is intended to be lived.

When they hurled their insults at him, he did not retaliate; when he suffered, he made no threats. Instead, he entrusted himself to him who judges justly. (1 Peter 2:23)

His secret was that he determined that he would not be the judge; he would relinquish that task to his Father, and he was certain that his Father would judge justly. Instead, he would love and serve.

In contrast, when you get angry, you are usually a vigilante party of one: judge, jury, and executioner. You are saying, "God, I don't trust you to give that person what he or she deserves, so I am going to play god on this one."

List at least a handful of resentments—times when you were angry or hurt—when the problem was, at least in part, your own pride and selfishness.

Can you see how you were trying to manage your own kingdom rather than trusting God?

As you get healthier, you will hunger for more skill and wisdom in relationships. Here is practical wisdom that will serve you well:

[Jesus said] "Why do you look at the speck of sawdust in your brother's eye and pay no attention to the plank in your own eye? How can you say to your brother, 'Let me take the speck out of your eye,' when all the time there is a plank in your own eye? You hypocrite, first take the plank out of your own eye, and then you will see clearly to remove the speck from your brother's eye." (Matthew 7:3–5)

Look at yourself before you judge others. Only then will you have the appropriate humility to talk about the other person's fault.

? How would you apply this teaching?

You are learning about life in the kingdom. It is different from life in the world. It serves rather than condemns. It forgives rather than accuses. It is not easier than ordinary life in the world, but it is so much better. Life in the kingdom is the way God intended you to live. When you live with the cross in view, forgiveness, service, and peace all make sense. You don't have to be defensive. Keep practicing, and it will gradually become more and more natural.

Now look at your list of hurts and resentments. Is it a shorter list?

> What started out as a way to get on top of addiction has become a course in the table manners of the Kingdom of God. Your friends are getting more than they thought. The kingdom way of life won't feel natural at first. But when you view life through the cross, it will all make sense.

Hurt from others' sins. The story, of course, is not over. Yes, some of your hurts have been intensified by your own sin, and you need to deal with that. But you also feel hurts that aren't your fault—hurts that have been caused by other people. God takes your hurt very seriously (Isaiah 40:11; Jeremiah 23:1–4). Jesus Christ was treated unjustly, and he has a unique affection for those who have been sinned against by other people. When he sees hurt, he comes close, like a shepherd to his sheep. He picks up those whose wounds are especially deep, speaks words of comfort, and reminds us that there will be justice. He mourns with those who mourn. He is carrying you.

> The LORD is close to the brokenhearted
>   and saves those who are crushed in spirit. (Psalm 34:18)

Can you see how important it is to begin with Jesus Christ when you are thinking about your relationships? He says much more than "forgive and forget." Without him you have no direction or hope, only pain and anger. With him you can find comfort and mercy that will outweigh the pain of your past.

But why hasn't he done something about the pain and injustice already? If you wonder about that, join the crowd—even Scripture writers asked that question. God's answer is that he *is* bringing justice; oppressors die and their evil dies with them. He also says that he will bring complete justice when he returns. Beyond that, we are not privy to the details. Instead, we are asked to trust him and receive the comfort he gives in the midst of the pain. He is God, both loving and powerful. You can trust that he will do what is right.

If you are looking for answers to all the pain in your life, God points you to the cross.

> Very rarely will anyone die for a righteous man, though for a good man someone might possibly dare to die. But God demonstrates his own love for us in this: While we were still sinners, Christ died for us. (Romans 5:7–8)

This changes everything. It brings comfort and humility. Someone suffered for you even when you were his enemy. If you really grasp this, you won't try to punish your enemies. Instead, you will consider how to treat them the way God has treated you.

> Do not repay anyone evil for evil. Be careful to do what is right in the eyes of everybody. If it is possible, as far as it depends on you, live at peace with everyone. Do not take revenge, my friends, but leave room for God's wrath, for it is written: "It is mine to avenge; I will repay," says the Lord. On the contrary: "If your enemy is hungry, feed him; if he is thirsty, give him something to drink. In doing this, you will heap burning coals on his head." Do not be overcome by evil, but overcome evil with good.
> (Romans 12:17–21)

Since love can take many forms, here again you need wisdom from others to figure out what real love looks like in different situations. For example, there are two basic ways to deal with the sins of your enemies. One is to overlook or "cover" them because, ultimately, sin is against

God and you are not the judge (1 Peter 4:8). The other way is to talk to the person who sinned against you, and to do it with grace and mercy. As a general rule, the closer the relationship, the more you will talk about how you have been hurt. Either way, the goal is to restore the relationship. The goal is love.

What you are doing now is going through the process of forgiving others. You are releasing the debt someone owes you and choosing to forgive as you have been forgiven.

Costly? Absolutely.

An opportunity and privilege? Yes, absolutely. You are walking in the footsteps of Jesus, and that is a humbling but exhilarating place to walk.

? Are you hopeful, or is this discouraging? Why?

RELATIONSHIPS IN WHICH YOU HAVE HURT OTHERS

Now for the part you have been expecting. You *have been sinned against* by others; you also *have sinned against* others. You are working on forgiving; now you also have to ask for forgiveness.

Where do you start? For some, the list is long. A complete list of those you have hurt is probably impossible to compile. Start with the person closest to you. If you can humble yourself, ask for forgiveness, and seek peace with that person, you will be able to do it with others.

? What did you do to that person? How did you sin against him or her? Look for anger, broken promises, blaming, deception and lies, and indifference and avoidance.

Now identify what lies at the root of some of these things. For example,

You loved yourself more than anyone else.
You loved your desires more than anyone and anything.
You were selfish and proud.

Since all your problems in relationships are even more deeply rooted in your sin against God, confess these things to him. You have cast aside his way of doing relationships, choosing to play god rather than live for him. Once you confess all that to God, confessing to a mere mortal should be easier.

Have you confessed the sins in your relationships to God?

There is still one more thing to do before you talk to the offended person. It's important to confess that your sin was against God, but it's also important to grasp that the cross announces your forgiveness. Even more than that, the cross of Jesus announces that God takes *joy* in forgiving you.

> You might have considered this passage earlier, but it is worth repeating. This time the group might want to add their sense of shame to the story. Every addict knows shame—the sense that you are unclean and a disgrace. Have them reflect on their shame. Then read this passage aloud as your gift to them. It should surprise.

"Suppose one of you has a hundred sheep and loses one of them. Does he not leave the ninety-nine in the open country and go after the lost sheep until he finds it? And when he finds it, he joyfully puts it on his shoulders and goes home. Then he calls his friends and neighbors together and says, 'Rejoice with me; I have found my lost sheep.' I tell you that in the same way there will be more rejoicing in heaven over one sinner who repents than over ninety-nine righteous persons who do not need to repent."

(Luke 15:4–7)

Do you believe this? God experiences joy because of *your* confession. If you don't believe it, don't move on yet. This is an important link in the chain, and you can't skip it. If you have a difficult time believing that God could do such a thing, you are close to understanding how amazing forgiveness really is. It *really is* amazing! It *is* hard to believe. Yet it is true. Remember, God is not like us. When he forgives with joy, he demonstrates that he is holy. He stands out above everything else in creation. Your task is to simply believe. Just believe that God said this to you, and believe that God only speaks the truth.

> Yet this also makes sense. The character of God can be seen in every-
> day life. For example, if your friends had a wayward child who they
> deeply loved, wouldn't they be excited when he returned? Wouldn't it
> be easy to put the past behind? When we as mere mortals occasion-
> ally do such things, we are pointing to what God does all the time.

No need to wallow in shame and self-loathing. Just respond with gratefulness, and let your love for Jesus grow. The rule is basic: If you are forgiven for much, you will love more.

Jesus answered him, "Simon, I have something to tell you."
"Tell me, teacher," he said.
"Two men owed money to a certain moneylender. One owed him five hundred denarii, and the other fifty. Neither of them had the money to pay him back, so he canceled the debts of both. Now which of them will love him more?"
Simon replied, "I suppose the one who had the bigger debt canceled."
"You have judged correctly," Jesus said. (Luke 7:40–43)

When you have received God's joyful and generous forgiveness, you are ready to go to the offended person. The process is simple.

Confess: "I have been looking at what I have done, and I know I am still missing a lot, but I have been so wrong in what I did to you."
Be specific: "I know that the last time we spoke I attacked you. My attack was my own defensiveness and a way to avoid my own sin."
Seek reconciliation: "If you are able, I want to seek your forgiveness and ask how I can reconcile with you."

At least the process is simple on paper! Simple isn't always easy. You might be walking into a firestorm, but if you have *any* questions on how to proceed, get help. Ask a wise friend or a pastor to help you with your strategy for reconciliation. Ask them to pray for you.

TAKE ACTION

There is plenty to do in this step. You could spend months on it. You can work on a small step right now, another tomorrow, and another the next day. After a month or two you will look back and notice genuine growth.

Keep short accounts. Are you frustrated with someone? Don't bury it. Someday it will come out as a craving for your addiction.

> You might want to highlight this: bad relationships, left to stew and ferment, end in cravings.

Forgive, and then decide if you should actually talk to the person. The prayer that Jesus gave us is, "Forgive us our debts [sins] as we also have forgiven our debtors [those who sinned against us]" (Matthew 6:12).

In a similar way, if you are in someone's debt because of your sin, deal with it as soon as you can. Don't think there will be a better time than now.

? What will you do?

Set out to be an expert in relationships. Relationships take humility and practice. If you don't have any models of good relationships in your life, you will feel like you are just making it up as you go along. So find out what Scripture says about relationships. Ask wise people how they do relationships, and ask them about good books on the subject. Watch good relationships in action.

? Who will you ask who can give you more wisdom in relationships?

What are you learning from the Bible about relationships? The universe is intensely relational. That is the way God made it. As a result, you could open your Bible at random and find something helpful. If you want to be more orderly, start reading through Ephesians and look for what it teaches you about your relationship with God and with other people.

Pray. Here is a paraphrase of Paul's relationship guidelines from Ephesians 4:29–5:2. You can use it as a prayer.

> Lord, you are the God of unity. You brought together the two most different groups in the world—Jews and

Gentiles—and you made them one. If this is the way your Spirit changes relationships, I need your Spirit. I want to love so that people know that you came in the flesh and are truly God.

Here is my desire:

to not let unwholesome words come out of my mouth;

to say only what is helpful for building up others;

to get rid of bitterness, anger, slander and anything else that
    breaks relationships;

to be kind and compassionate;

to forgive as I have been forgiven; and

to imitate you and live a life of love.

Does anyone want to pronounce a blessing on the group? Here is one: *You are not your own; you are bought with a price. May you spend the rest of your life becoming more and more amazed that Jesus did this for you.*

Respond Well When You Go Wrong

MAIN IDEA: When you take steps backward, back to your addiction, you don't have to end up where you started. How you respond to failure is as important as knowing the next step forward. The key is to get to Jesus Christ as quickly as possible.

> Most addicts have, at some point, **said** "no" to addiction and **done** "yes." Even worse, they might have said "no" publicly, which made the "yes" a more obvious failure. Such failures can be deadly. They lead to guilt, shame, hopelessness, and a reason to reunite with the old addictive object. The addicts feel miserable, so they might as well do something that gives voice to their misery. And what says misery better than addiction and its many consequences?
>
> The goal is to be an imitator of Jesus—to be truly human, as the Father intended. This doesn't happen all at once. The path of sanctification is a bumpy one. Remember that our Father values the way we get to the goal as well as the goal itself.

To succeed, you must learn how to fail. Every business owner and every wise person will tell you that. You might occasionally hear a Patton-esque speech such as, "Failure is not an option," but everyone experiences failure. The difference between the wise and the foolish is that the wise learn from their failures.

The standard pattern for failure is well known. You muster up the best intentions to avoid your addiction. Enough is enough! You are hurting others and you know that what you are doing is wrong, so you make up your mind to stop. But then, somehow, it just happens, like a horrible accident. You are driving along, minding your own business, when all of a sudden you find yourself regaining consciousness and your car is totaled.

When you are really trying to avoid addiction but relapse anyway, it's easy to give up all hope and fall back to where you started. After reviving that addictive relationship, rarely does anyone stop at only one pill, drink, porn site, or whatever the addiction is. One more leads to one more. Then the guilt kicks in, so you want to medicate it away, and the only means that comes to mind is your addiction—you indulge some more. Then you think about how you are letting others down, so you feel more guilty and miserable, and you need even more of your addiction to numb yourself. Finally, hopelessness is in full bloom. "Who cares? Nothing matters now anyway." You are in freefall.

You don't even want to think about your relationship with God. You don't want to face him. You feel as if you can't even think about talking to him until you have climbed out of the abyss and set off on the right path again, and that could take quite a while. If you are honest, you might also notice a hint of anger. You feel as if God could have honored your good intentions with more help—at least he could have stopped your long fall much earlier.

You have probably been there.

? What pattern does your relapse follow?

WHAT HAPPENED?

Right away, let's put to rest the myth about God.

> When tempted, no one should say, "God is tempting me." For God cannot be tempted by evil, nor does he tempt anyone; but each one is tempted when, by his own evil desire, he is dragged away and enticed. Then, after desire has conceived, it gives birth to sin; and sin, when it is full-grown, gives birth to death.
>
> (James 1:13–15)

Step 1 in failing well is refusing to blame God. The problem is that you love the object of your old addiction more than you hate it. You still desire it. What felt like a sudden crash actually had a history to it.

Here are the usual suspects. Check the ones that sound familiar.

— You got cocky. There wasn't daily, desperate dependence on God and others. You forgot you were in a battle.

— You purposefully left the door ajar so your addiction could return.

— Your imagination was thinking back fondly to your old addiction.

— Your plan was reduced to little more than, "Try not to do it."

— You believed lies about God. You doubted his care, his goodness, and his power.

— You thought it was unfair that you had to avoid your addiction while other people could moderately indulge or weren't even tempted. (Anytime you think something is unfair, you are saying God is unfair. You are judging him and saying you deserve better.)

— You believed lies about yourself: either you thought you were way too good or way too bad.

— You experienced pain, fear, anger, or guilt. Instead of turning to Jesus and other people, you turned to your addiction for comfort.

Anything you want to add to the pattern of how you are "dragged away and enticed" (James 1:14)?

GET TO THE HEART OF THE MATTER

By now you know that you are linked to God in everything you do. Work, play, relationships—you are either running from him or toward him. When you relapsed, you were running from him. You probably didn't realize it at the time. Remember, you don't necessarily have conscious thoughts about God before and during your relapse, though you might. Addiction and blindness go hand in hand. When you are going back to your addiction, you don't see spiritual reality because you are running away from God. All you see is that object of your affection.

Keep learning from past failures. Why did you follow your own path, even though it was destructive? You can plead insanity, which would be accurate as far as it goes, but your insanity had its reasons. What lies did you believe? How did the cross of Jesus Christ—the proof of God's goodness and love—gradually fade, if in fact it was ever vivid and central in the first place? Be specific and honest with yourself.

Assume that you replayed the scene from the Garden of Eden (Genesis 2–3). The serpent baited you with questions about God, and you took the bait.

You believed that God was not altogether good. You thought that anyone who puts a fence around an attractive tree and says you can't eat from it must be stingy. You thought God must be trying to keep you from having a good time.

There is the selfishness.

You believed that you could rest in your own knowledge rather than what God had said. God said, "Don't eat from the tree"; you knew better.

There is the pride.

Are you getting into the habit of tracing your actions back to your kingdom allegiances?

CONFESS AND KNOW YOU ARE FORGIVEN

When you return to your addiction, you will eventually feel guilty—at least you should *hope* to feel guilty. Your guilt is a sign that you are still alive. You are able to hear God's words to you. Guilt is evidence that the Spirit is at work in your heart (John 16:8). Guilt is good; it is a warning light that says you need to turn to the Lord and confess your sin. He, of course, will be quick to forgive you.

> If we confess our sins, he is faithful and just and will forgive us our sins and purify us from all unrighteousness. (1 John 1:9)

The problem comes when you misinterpret that warning light to mean, "God is mad at me." You interpret it to mean that he is so disgusted he doesn't want to talk to you right now. You impose your own punishment; you stay out of his hair and go to bed without your supper. You decide you'd better not talk to him until you have figured out some way to get your life back on track.

It sounds spiritual: you feel bad, and you deserve punishment. But notice which way you are headed! You are turned away from God rather than toward him. In reality, you are on that same old path of pursuing your own kingdom. It might be difficult to see this at first, but you are back to managing the world your way. You don't believe that God loves, pursues, and invites you to come back. You don't believe that he is delighted when a sinner turns to him.

This is subtle and hard to detect, which means that it has Satan's fingerprints all over it.

If this is your situation, you have more to confess than you realize. Yes, you worshiped your desires and your addiction. Even more, you dealt with it on your own terms. You didn't turn back to the Lord and say, "Please have mercy on me, a sinner." That is the path of humility. Instead, you tried to make things right, as though you had the power to do such a thing. You have vastly overestimated your ability to pay God back, and you have severely underestimated his love and mercy.

> This is legalism. It is targeted especially in the Book of Galatians. Legalism is that old sinful instinct that says we can and must contribute to our standing before God. The apostle Paul is ruthless in his criticism of this behavior because the glory of God is at stake. He sees legalism for what it is—a form of pride that won't acknowledge that Jesus Christ has done everything for us.

There it is again: selfishness and pride. You can find it everywhere. Guilt that doesn't turn to God strangles all spiritual growth. Your task, then, is a lifelong search-and-destroy mission for sin *and* guilt.

Such guilt can masquerade in many forms:

"I can't believe that God would forgive me."

"Maybe God can forgive me, but I can't forgive myself."

"I will have to try harder next time to show God I am sorry."

"I have fallen so many times, there is no point to asking God's forgiveness *again*."

What forms does guilt take in you?

> You are likely to hear, "Maybe God can forgive me, but I can't forgive myself." On the one hand, it might be an addict's way to describe shame. He or she believes they are forgiven, but they still feel unclean and unacceptable. If this is the case, then you can assure your brothers or sisters that the blood of Christ is powerful enough to cleanse us from both guilt and shame. If you move into this conversation, you will want people to identify what they mean by shame.
>
> But there is another way to interpret "I can't forgive myself." Listen carefully and you might hear pride rather than humility. Humility believes what the Lord says. Pride questions the words of God. Pride actually stands over God's words and says that the final court of appeals rests in our own judgment rather than his.

Whatever form it takes, attack it. Confess your sin. Then get to the hard part. Don't move on until you have inklings of joy and a greater love for the One who forgave you. The process of being forgiven can't end with your bad feelings. It must end with an acknowledgment of God's holiness and love. He doesn't treat you as your sins deserve.

Try it. Talk to someone else about how this is done. You are not minimizing your sin; your joy is a statement about how great God is.

What about confessing to other people? You know the drill. What you confess to God you will also confess to those who were affected by your relapse. Make the confession as public as the crime. If it was private and no one knew about it, be sure to acknowledge it to at least one other person. You want to keep your life in the light—in public—when possible.

REFINE YOUR PLAN

Your plan was less foolproof than you thought. As a way to be better prepared, write it out.

> Different addictions attract different kinds of people. Some types of addicts, such as people with eating disorders, write easily. Others, such as drug addicts and alcoholics, rely more on the spoken word than the written. Use your judgment on this, but if your friend has the ability to write, push him or her to write.

What happened? Why did I fall?

What have I learned from this so I don't have to repeat it?

What is my improved plan?

Where is Jesus in my plan?

Show this to people you trust. Ask for their comments. Do they see any loopholes?

Your plan should be specific and doable. Don't get too grandiose on this one. You know enough about yourself and what you will do and what you won't do.

"I will read ten chapters of the Bible every day and spend a half hour praying."

"I will never think about my addiction again."

Those sound good and they might impress others, but if you have never done those things before, what makes you think you will start now? You don't want a plan you know will fail before you finish writing it.

You are not doing this to please other people. You are doing it because you are in great danger, because sin is wreaking havoc in the lives of people around you, and, most importantly, because the Lord of the universe has spoken. Follow him, live under his lordship and for his glory, and resist the enemy who is trying to sabotage your life.

You have changed loyalties. You are learning how to turn from your selfish ways and live under the protection and authority of the true King. You lost a skirmish, but you aren't going to lose the war.

? Hope check: Do you have hope? Why? Why not?

Where is your hope, from 1 to 10?

1	2	3	4	5	6	7	8	9	10
Hopelessness									Hope

GUERILLA WARFARE: THE ADVANCED COURSE

Scripture doesn't talk that often about Satan. Of the anti-God triumvirate of our sinful desires, our idols, and the devil, it focuses more on our own sinful desires. But make no mistake, Satan is on the prowl. When you relapse, it is time to keep the enemy in view.

The world you live in is in conflict. Battles are around you and within you. To make things more difficult, the enemy is hard to locate. Unlike the warfare of centuries past, when uniforms clearly identified the enemy who stood opposite you in crisp, obvious lines, here you are stalked by an enemy whose tactics are exclusively those of guerilla warfare.

Satan uses stealth and lies. He is camouflaged as an angel of light (2 Corinthians 11:14). With a few, seemingly innocent questions, he can spin you around: "Your circumstances seem very difficult. Is God really good?"

When everything is going well and you are dealing quickly with sin in your life, Satan patiently waits. He doesn't see any vulnerability at that moment, but he suspects he will. He is waiting for one of two things: guilt or hardship. At the first evidence of guilt, he races in. He is the accuser (Revelation 12:10). He knows that your guilt can separate you from the Lord as long as he can convince you that your wrongness is greater than God's willingness to forgive. While he accuses you, he also subtly accuses God. Just listen for accusations that make God out to be like an ordinary person:

> "Why would God forgive you again, especially after you vowed never to do what you just did?"
>
> "He must be awfully mad at you. Leave him alone for a while. Give him some time to cool off."

Hardship, too, is Satan's call to arms. Remember how Satan assumed that suffering in Job's life would cause him to turn away from God? Satan made that assumption because, from his vantage point, it was a natural law for human beings. When everything is good, you worship God. When life is difficult, you turn from him. Job was one of the few exceptions.

Because you don't see yourself as the one-in-a-million person that Job was, that natural law can be very intimidating. But Satan isn't telling you the whole story. Job lived before Jesus came. The Spirit of God had not been given to human beings in the same way he is now. God had made promises of new hearts and new strength to follow him, but the fulfillment of those promises was still a few centuries away.

Everything changed after Jesus rose from the dead and ascended to heaven. Once he was seated on his throne, his first kingly act was to send the Spirit to his people (Acts 1–2). Suddenly, suffering became a time when people turned *to* God rather than away from him.

> Consider it pure joy, my brothers, whenever you face trials of many kinds, because you know that the testing of your faith develops perseverance. Perseverance must finish its work so that you may be mature and complete, not lacking anything. (James 1:2–4)

This is the new law. If Jesus suffered, the people God loves could also expect to suffer. But with the Spirit of Jesus within them, suffering will strengthen rather than break them.

You know that difficulties in your life—depression, rejection, memories of abuse, financial problems—have been an invitation to your addiction. Now you understand why. Satan rushes in with his lies during those difficulties. When times are good, you might be less prone to believe Satan's lies, but when times are tough, they sound like truth.

? Revisit the connection between suffering and addiction in your life. How have you turned away from God during suffering and become more vulnerable to your addiction as a result?

? Do you know how to turn to God during hardships? Can you think of times when suffering placed you at the crossroads and you turned *to* Jesus rather than away from him?

No matter how well you deal with hardships in your life, growth here will be a lifelong project.

TAKE ACTION

The action steps should sound more and more like reminders.

Do you have hope?

Why?

Are you feeding on Scripture yet?

What do you pray?

Are you learning the skill of being able to turn quickly to Jesus? If you know anything about him, you know he embraces those who turn to him. Even if you have walked miles down the path of your own desires, you can still turn quickly toward Jesus. The amazing reality is that, no matter how far you run from him, he is right there whenever you turn. You never have to make a long walk back by yourself.

Are you learning how to go through hardships without the help of your addiction? Think of yourself as a toddler when it comes to responding to hardships. You have spent much of your life escaping them. As a result, you missed a God-given means of growing up. That's why some addicts seem emotionally younger than their chronological age. Maturity, character, wisdom—they are all forged by hardships.

> Addicts are like most Americans. They believe they have a right to happiness. When happiness is absent, they feel justified in finding it in other ways. Scripture counters with perseverance. It is not a gift we always want, but it is one of the best. If you really want to be more like your heavenly Father, learn perseverance.

Time to get good and mad. The accuser—the devil—assumes that you will always fall down when hard times come. Defy him by setting out on a course in which, good times and bad, you will be *certain* that the cross of Jesus proves God's love for you. In humility, which Satan hates, you will remember that you are a mere child who can't always understand how God uses suffering to build up his people. You acknowledge that God's love is more sophisticated than you can understand.

You are certainly not alone in this battle. For encouragement, you can pick up almost any book in the New Testament and read how God's people responded to suffering. The Book of 1 Peter is one letter that is all about how to live while suffering.

Hundreds of good books are available too. Ask your pastor for his favorite book on suffering.

> How do you want to bless the people in your group? What benediction—literally, "good words"—do you want to give them? And don't forget to give others the opportunity to pronounce a blessing.

Welcome to the Banquet

MAIN IDEA: When you lose hope, you give up. You think nothing will help. For change to continue, you must be ready to give reasons for your hope at a moment's notice.

This step is a demanding one. You are grappling with critical spiritual realities. Unless the Spirit of God impresses them on the heart, these stories will seem like nothing more than old fables with no connection to the trials of life. As a result, though group times have already been filled with prayer, your prayer should be more urgent, more desperate.

The steps we've covered in this book have a logical order, and this one is both a next step and a summary of the others. For example, in Step 2 you considered why you wanted to change. One reason that question is so important is that it reveals where you have put your hope. Children, jobs, spouses, parents, personal health—these are all good reasons to change, but they can't be **the** reason. They are not strong enough to prop up your hopes when you are in the desert. Put your deepest hope in anything other than Jesus, and your plans will crumble.

Notice also that you are still revising your story. Now you are more focused on the character of God, and you are making the connection between what Jesus did in history and how you live right now. You are laying out the reasons why we get up after we fall rather than just stay defeated. Step 10 brings these things together and adds some details.

Hopelessness and despair are natural reactions when you have been defeated over and over. As your group meets, acknowledge that fact. But in this step we bring that despair out into the open. Yes, despair is a natural response to multiple defeats. But it is also much more than that; it is also a sign that spiritual war is raging. All hopelessness has Satan's fingerprints all over it. He emphasizes our failed plans and strained relationships. His strategy is to drown out the hope we find in what Jesus has already done.

Get tough with this. This is something—and someone—to get angry with. In contrast, every single step toward and in the kingdom of God is filled with hope. You are entitled to hope as God's child not because you earned it, but because God has given it to you in Christ. If there is no evidence of hope in your life, you are going the wrong way. Insist on hope.

This hope comes alive in the larger story of what God has done. Emphasize that this story is highly accessible—anyone can understand it. It can make sense. To make it our own, all it takes is prayerful listening. But don't listen superficially and let it roll off your back. It will come alive in our hearts as we pray for the Spirit to brand us with the truth. Then we study it and ask questions when we don't understand. We make an effort to meditate on it and let it penetrate our hearts.

> "These commandments that I give you today are to be upon your hearts. Impress them on your children. Talk about them when you sit at home and when you walk along the road, when you lie down and when you get up. Tie them as symbols on your hands and bind them on your foreheads. Write them on the doorframes of your houses and on your gates."
> (Deuteronomy 6:6–9)

Hope is the conviction that the battle is worth it. There is a reason for all the work. Somehow, the story will end well.

In sports you hear announcers say that a team has momentum, which means that the players are making an extra effort because they think victory is within reach. They have hope. The team has been inspired by a coach's speech, an extraordinary effort by a teammate, or a hint of fatigue in the opposing team. Hope keeps you moving through the difficult times.

It is not positive thinking, and it is much more than a personal desire or wish, as in, "I hope I get a new bike for Christmas." With addictions, hope is the confidence that a good, effective plan exists. To put it more personally, it is the confidence that God himself will be with you, and he has prepared a banquet that is better than anything you could imagine.

Without this hope, you are left wandering aimlessly until you finally realize the futility of it all. Then you give up. But with true hope, nothing can stop you.

? Do you have hope? What keeps you going through the tough times?

Hope is always hope *in* someone or something. You hope in something to rescue or save you. At one time your hope was in your addiction, even if you would have never put it in those terms. You thought it would be your savior in difficult times, but it wasn't enough. It betrayed you. Your addiction couldn't sustain your hope.

Everything you have done up to this point has been intended to transfer your hope from your addiction to someone much sturdier and better—Jesus the King.

Where are you in that process?

? What are some of the signs that say your hope is shifting from your addictive ways to Jesus?

In order to secure whatever progress you have made, and to continue to grow, hope is essential. You must have a ready answer when your cravings come full force and misery hits you hard. At those times you must be able to put into words why you bother to follow Jesus. After all, you can gladly follow Jesus when you feel as if he is giving you everything you want. It is when you can't see obvious evidence of God's goodness that you must walk with hope.

One way you have already nurtured hope is by retelling your story. You can see the place where the paths diverge. You know that the two paths lead to two very different kingdoms, which at first glance look equally appealing. In fact, at first the path *away* from God's kingdom is the one that seems most attractive.

Each step you have taken so far has been intended to make you more discerning at that decision point. You know you must choose carefully. What looks good might actually be bad. You are hungry, and food is in sight only a short distance down the dangerous path. At one time your hunger ruled. It was simple: you were hungry and food was available. Now, however, you are savvier. You pause and detect the smell of poison. You notice that a trap has been set to spring as soon as you touch it. So you follow the path where there are promises of a true banquet, even though you don't quite see it.

Now add more detail to your story. It will help when you are hungry and feeling desperate. The details can give you more hope and encouragement in the journey.

THE BIBLE TELLS *YOUR* STORY

When you tell your story, remember that much of it has already been told. Your story is written down in the Bible.

As you know, the story has a rough beginning. After initial signs of hope in a beautiful garden, everything went dark.

The story picks up when God liberated the children of Israel from Egypt with his powerful hand. They were set free *not* because they were stronger or morally superior to the Egyptians. They were set free simply because God was faithful to the promises he had made to Abraham— that the entire world would be blessed through his family tree.

Once Israel was liberated, you might think the people would have been forever grateful, giving no thought to any other gods. After all, God had shown his superiority over the strongest kingdom of the world and its collection of gods—no more competition, no one else to worship. But human beings are fickle creatures who prefer independence and idolatry. Within days of their dramatic deliverance, the Israelites were complaining, pining for the days of their slavery, erecting other gods, and letting their lusts run amok.

In response to the people's rebellion, God placed a temporary roadblock between them and the land he promised them. The roadblock was as much for training as it was for their chastisement. The people were only going to be able to enter the new land if they trusted in God alone. The forty-year detour in the desert taught them how to live by the words of God instead of by their own desires.

All this should be sounding familiar and personal. This is your story.

Your crossroad is in the same desert. You aren't walking down a lovely country path when you notice that the paths diverge. You are in the desert; you are parched and famished. This is where spiritual battle is waged. The heat of life—the disappointments, pain, and loss—is searing. You are being tested. Will you turn to God, or will you turn to your own devices?

> Remember how the LORD your God led you all the way in the desert these forty years, to humble you and to test you in order to know what was in your heart, whether or not you would keep his commands. He humbled you, causing you to hunger and then feeding you with manna . . . to teach you that man does not live on bread alone but on

every word that comes from the mouth of the LORD. (Deuteronomy 8:2–3)

The Israelites' track record during these tests or temptations was wretched. They actually got worse over time. By the end of the Old Testament, hope is a mere spark. It looks as though the dark kingdom has won, the human heart will be forever prone to wander from God, and we have no hope of change.

A prophet foresaw this darkness:

Distressed and hungry, they will roam through the land; when they are famished, they will become enraged and, looking upward, will curse their king and their God. Then they will look toward the earth and see only distress and darkness and fearful gloom, and they will be thrust into utter darkness. (Isaiah 8:21–22)

But the story was not over. God is faithful even when we are not. He made promises that the Messiah would come and change everything. And God always keeps his promises. With this in mind, the same prophet who predicted doom and gloom pressed on to hope. Look at this glorious "Nevertheless":

Nevertheless, there will be no more gloom for those who were in distress. In the past he humbled the land of Zebulun and the land of Naphtali, but in the future he will honor Galilee of the Gentiles, by the way of the sea, along the Jordan—

The people walking in darkness
   have seen a great light;
on those living in the land of the shadow of death
   a light has dawned.
You have enlarged the nation
   and increased their joy;
they rejoice before you
   as people rejoice at the harvest,
as men rejoice
   when dividing the plunder. . . .

For to us a child is born,
    to us a son is given,
    and the government will be on his shoulders.
And he will be called
    Wonderful Counselor, Mighty God,
    Everlasting Father, Prince of Peace. (Isaiah 9:1–3, 6)

When invading armies overran the Hebrew nation, they entered through Zebulun and Naphtali. Jesus was an invader too. He began his ministry on earth in Zebulun and Naphtali. But before he brought light to these places, he had something else to do. The King's first official act on earth was to go out into the wilderness—the place of temptations—where *everyone* had failed before him. Furthermore, the heat was going to be turned up even more, and Jesus knew it. While God gave bread to the Israelites, Jesus went without food for forty days.

Cravings? Temptations? He was maxed out. No one had a harder time.

Satan, of course, was lying in wait in the wilderness. That certainly isn't surprising. He is always looking for an easy mark, and a place of hardship is a good place to find one. Jesus was God in the flesh, but Jesus' hardships were so intense, Satan thought he might win this one. Satan knew the law at work in most humans: the more severe the trials, the easier it is to draw that person away from the kingdom of God.

The battle was on.

Then Jesus was led by the Spirit into the desert to be tempted by the devil. After fasting forty days and forty nights, he was hungry. The tempter came to him and said, "If you are the Son of God, tell these stones to become bread."

Jesus answered, "It is written: 'Man does not live on bread alone, but on every word that comes from the mouth of God.'"

Then the devil took him to the holy city and had him stand on the highest point of the temple. "If you are the Son of God," he said, "throw yourself down. For it is written: 'He will command his angels concerning you, and they will lift you up in their hands, so that you will not strike your foot against a stone.'"

Jesus answered him, "It is also written: 'Do not put the Lord your God to the test.'"

Again, the devil took him to a very high mountain and showed him all the kingdoms of the world and their splendor. "All this I will give you," he said, "if you will bow down and worship me."

Jesus said to him, "Away from me, Satan! For it is written: 'Worship the Lord your God, and serve him only.'" (Matthew 4:1–10)

What does this have to do with you? Everything. Your story is being rewritten. In your place Jesus went out into the wilderness—the place of temptations and difficulties. He was offered physical satisfaction and earthly kingdoms if he would only engage in a moment of false worship. He said no.

All history, and certainly every addict, had been waiting for this event. Would anyone *ever* choose God over themselves when temptations were at their strongest? It didn't look promising. Then, in the middle of human history, the Son of God came and did what we could never do.

Go back further for only a minute. This story of temptations actually goes from Adam to Israel to Jesus. The first wilderness was actually a hospitable garden. Adam and Eve were the ones who faced the temptation. When Adam gave in to Satan's temptation, he sealed the fate of everyone who followed him (Genesis 3; Romans 5:12–19). Adam was our representative, and he failed the test. If you are going to get out of bondage, someone has to pass the test on your behalf.

When Jesus went out into the wilderness, he was the second Adam, the representative for Israel and for all humankind. He went out to accomplish what no one else could, and he did it. He passed the test in our place. And when he went to the cross, his sinlessness made it possible for him to be the sacrifice for *our* sins.

When you have a representative or substitute, your fortunes are tied to that person. Your ambassador makes a treaty, and it is your treaty. Your king declares war, and you are at war. When Jesus, your representative, went out into the desert, his victory became yours.

How do the actions of Jesus become yours? They become yours when you trust and follow him. Whoever you trust in is your lord. Trust the King, and you get the kingdom. When he wins, you win.

Does it sound strange? It shouldn't. Examples of it are everywhere. When you marry someone, you take on your spouse's story—and reputation and debts and everything else. When you are adopted into a new family, you take on the family's story. When you declare your allegiance to a king, you inherit an entirely new history and future.

The history of Israel is your story. More importantly, the story of Jesus is also your story.

> Up to this point you have led your brothers or sisters in refining their story so it fits God's telling of it. You have added features like "voluntary" and idolatry. You have emphasized that every story is connected to our spiritual allegiances. Now what you have done, by way of the history of Israel, is take these stories one more step. Now you are watching the unfolding story of Scripture and saying, "That's me; that's my story!"
>
> All along we have been trying to make connections between Scripture and your friends' lives. This step says that Scripture does not only inform the telling of our story; it is our story. As a result, every page of Scripture is poised to come alive because it is about us. This is a mouthful, but it is important that your friends be brought into this story in such a way that it becomes their story. If they don't understand something, stop and seek God's wisdom so you can understand together.

HOPE WHEN TEMPTED

Jesus' story is your story. That explains how you are forgiven when you did nothing to deserve it. Because Jesus represented you, his life changes your record and his death pays the penalty for your sin. You are no longer condemned when you stumble and fall. But there is more. God did not bring you into his kingdom so you could keep falling when tested. He brought you so you would look more like him. To make that happen, he gave you his Spirit, the Spirit of Jesus Christ.

Now when you are in the desert, you are not alone. You have the record of Jesus, and you also have his power to resist and flee temptations. You no longer *have* to give in to temptation. Everything really has changed.

No temptation has seized you except what is common to man. And God is faithful; he will not let you be tempted beyond what you can bear. But when you are tempted, he will also provide a way out so that you can stand up under it. Therefore, my dear friends, flee from idolatry. (1 Corinthians 10:13–14)

Could you imagine a better hope? Temptations will certainly come. They will come at you fast and furious, when you are in the desert and feeling weak. But now, instead of certain defeat and mindless idolatry, there is a way out. You don't have to say yes to your temptations! You can actually flee them. New power is in the new kingdom.

Let's say you enjoy a particular computer game. People who know you are a little surprised at your devotion to it. Defeat after defeat, you keep playing. Do you know why? Because the game promises that there is a way to win. If the game had no solution, you wouldn't even try. But you know that practice will lead you to the answer, so you persevere.

Every problem is like that. If there is hope for a solution—if you are certain of it—you are more likely to hang in there until you get it.

There is work ahead. The promise—the hope—is not a promise of ease but a promise of power. In Christ you have new power, a new story, and a new outcome. But old ways die hard, and they don't go without a fight. That's the way God has ordered human life. He blesses the diligent, faithful work of his children, whether the work is farming a field, learning a new skill, or resisting temptation. You had no reason to work before because all it did was postpone your relapse. But now, perhaps for the first time, you have reasons to get aggressive against your addiction. Life in God's kingdom is filled with purpose, and a banquet is set for you. It is just around the bend.

TAKE ACTION

Your hope, from 1 to 10?

1   2   3   4   5   6   7   8   9

10Hopelessness   Hope

Everything that was written in the past was written to teach us, so that through endurance and the encouragement of the Scriptures we might have hope. (Romans 15:4, emphasis added)

Do hope. If hope is lagging, feed it. Read Scripture, and ask the Spirit of God to give you the hope he promises. Indifference and inaction are not options. You can't make it if biblical stories of hope leave you unmoved. Without hope you are vulnerable. If you aren't pursuing it, you probably don't want it because it seals off the path to your addiction more than you want it to. Whatever the reason for your hopelessness, talk about it with someone else. Read this step aloud with another person, and stop at places that aren't penetrating your heart. In fact, stop and pray at those places. God wants to give you hope. You can have it—and if hope is growing, share it.

Study 1 Corinthians 10:13–14. Read the whole chapter. Talk about it with a friend.

Have you noticed that the Bible is not only helping you tell your story, but it *is* your story?

How is the Bible telling your story? Have you noticed that with each retelling of your story you are getting closer and closer to the way God tells it? Now try telling your story using God's story of humanity.

Expect temptations. Since you have power to flee temptations, you can actually look forward to the times when temptations come. Here is a passage that includes verses you have read before.

Consider it pure joy, my brothers, whenever you face trials of many kinds, because you know that the testing of your faith develops perseverance. Perseverance must finish its work so that you may be mature and complete, not lacking anything. . . . Blessed is the man who perseveres under trial, because when he has stood the test, he will receive the crown of life that God has promised to those who love him. When tempted, no one should say, "God is tempting me." For God cannot be tempted by evil, nor does he tempt anyone; but each one is tempted when, by his own evil desire, he is dragged away and enticed. Then, after desire has conceived, it gives birth to sin; and sin, when it is full-grown, gives birth to death. . . . Do not merely listen to the word, and so deceive yourselves. Do what it says. Anyone who listens to the word but does not do what it says is like a man who looks at his face in a mirror and, after looking at himself, goes away and immediately forgets what he looks like. But the man who looks intently into the perfect law that gives freedom, and continues to do this, not forgetting what he has heard, but doing it—he will be blessed in what he does. (James 1:2–4, 12–15, 22–25)

God assures you that you will be tempted again. He also promises that his Spirit will be with you at those times, and he will show you the way of escape. Take that way of escape once, and you will find it easier to do the next time.

Pray. Temptations mean that you will notice cravings again. Have you ever prayed, "Lord, please take away my cravings?" Here is a better way to pray.

"Our Father in heaven,
hallowed be your name,
your kingdom come,
your will be done
    on earth as it is in heaven.
Give us today our daily bread.
Forgive us our debts,
    as we also have forgiven our debtors.
And lead us not into temptation,
but deliver us from the evil one."
                            (Matthew 6:9–13)

The Lord's Prayer contains the essentials.

The kingdom is about God, not you.

You want the kingdom of heaven to continue to penetrate your heart as well as the world around you.

    You have real physical needs, so you ask that they be met.

    You have even deeper spiritual needs: to forgive and be forgiven.

You need strength to face temptation. "Lead us not into temptation" means "lead us not into temptation without your strength arming us in the battle. Then we will be delivered from the Evil One."

Growth is a lifelong walk; we repeat these steps again and again. The problem is not that we didn't get it the first time. The problem is that we easily forget reality and need the reminders. The problem is that we still prefer instant cures over long, arduous training. Yet God is pleased to bless our persistence. There **is** a banquet. We will taste it as we keep walking in the right direction, and we will keep receiving more. It will taste like peace, joy, contentment, and hope.

Let your hope pour out in a benediction.

AND REPEAT

As with "Getting Started," this can be a separate step by itself. It will be a nice break from the longer and more rigorous steps, and it should be. It has more of heaven in it. So enjoy it. Imagine it together. Talk about the beauty of the Lord. Anticipate the rest that is to come. Realize that we are given these good things right now in Jesus. **Today** he can be satisfying. **Today** he spreads out a banquet before us. Can your friends and, hopefully, brothers see those things? In Christ, we have already been given the kingdom and all its blessings, and the best is yet to come.

There you have it: wisdom that is accessible to a child yet powerful enough to destroy addictive strongholds. Certainly more could be said—the entire Bible speaks to you in particular—but you have the basic story. If you think there must be something more, pray that you would see even more reality.

And you need to repeat these steps for the rest of your life.

As you do, you will notice a change in your diet. You have been hungry and thirsty but for the wrong things. It's as if your diet was all junk food and it was killing you. Now you are developing an appetite for *real* food and *real* drink.

The food and drink is Jesus. He will satisfy you, and he will give you more even before you ask for it.

Whoever is thirsty, let him come; and whoever wishes, let him take the free gift of the water of life. (Revelation 22:17)

Jesus declared, "I am the bread of life. He who comes to me will never go hungry, and he who believes in me will never be thirsty." (John 6:35)

The way to choose the right path, the way to fight the battle, is to want something that is better than your addiction. Because your addiction can sometimes be quite attractive to you, only something else extraordinary will fit the bill. Jesus is, indeed, much better.

Here is a prayer that can be your new goal:

O God, you are my God,
    earnestly I seek you;
my soul thirsts for you,
    my body longs for you,
in a dry and weary land
    where there is no water.
I have seen you in the sanctuary
    and beheld your power and your glory.
Because your love is better than life,
    my lips will glorify you.
I will praise you as long as I live,
    and in your name I will lift up my hands.
My soul will be satisfied as with the richest of foods;
    with singing lips my mouth will praise you.
                              (Psalm 63:1–5)

So you have been invited.

"Come, all you who are thirsty,
    come to the waters;
and you who have no money,
    come, buy and eat!
Come, buy wine and milk
    without money and without cost.
Why spend money on what is not bread,
    and your labor on what does not satisfy?
Listen, listen to me, and eat what is good,
    and your soul will delight in the richest of fare."
                              (Isaiah 55:1–2)

This passage should be shocking. The only requirement is that you come with nothing. Don't bring your efforts to try harder or attempts to pay God back for all the trouble you have caused; just come with empty hands because Jesus Christ has paid for the banquet in full. In your discussion about this passage, consider both the residual human instinct toward legalism, and get specific about the "richest of fare." What is it, and how have you already tasted it?

Welcome to the banquet.
Welcome to the kingdom.